FortiGate
Troubleshooting Guide Quick Reference

Hubert Wiśniewski

About the Autor

Hubert Wiśniewski is a Principal Network Engineer at AT&T. He has been working in IT industry for 20 years and last 10 years with computer networks and security. He holds the following certifications: Fortinet NSE4 NSE5 NSE7, Cisco Certified Network Professional (CCNP) R&S Sec, Cisco Certified Design Professional (CCDP), CompTIA Network+ Security+. Hubert, as Fortinet Certified Trainer, delivers official Fortinet courses. He also developed FortiGate Bootcamp. Hubert is a member of Cisco Security Exam Advisory Group as Subject Matter Expert.

About the Technical Reviewers (alphabetical order)

Eduard Dulharu is a Senior Network Architect at AT&T for more than 6 years. He has more than 10 years of experience in designing, implementing and troubleshooting large scale networks for different industries and customers.

Efren Teruel Dominguez is a Senior Network Engineer at AT&T. He has been working with all life cycles of computer networks, like deployment, developing or troubleshooting. In past he worked for Amazon in Dublin and Seattle focusing on automation. He is a member of Cisco Service Provider Advisory Group as SME.

Giovanni Pagano Dritto is a Freelancer Network Consultant and programmer. He works in the IT industry for over 10 years and he has extensive work experience with a wide variety of network technologies and vendors. He is also an experienced Python Developer with a demonstrated history of working in different sectors of IT industry.

Lucian Lisov is a Senior Network Engineer at AT&T with over 10 years of experience. Specialized in enterprise data center infrastructures he devotes most of his time to private/public clouds and automation.

Warning, disclaimer, copyright, trademark, acknowledgments and errata

The information in the book is provided on an "as is" basis. The author disclaims all responsibility for errors or omissions, including without limitation responsibility for damages resulting from the use of the book.

The opinions expressed in this book belong to the author and are not necessarily those of Fortinet.

Copyright 2020 by Hubert Wiśniewski.

All Fortinet products and features described in the book are trademarks of Fortinet.

Errata: http://myitmicroblog.blogspot.com/2020/04/errata.html

About the Book

FortiGate – Troubleshooting Guide Quick Reference presents easy to understand techniques of troubleshooting on FortiGate platform. There are many debug command examples, which explain, how to read and understand the command output. The intention of the book is not to teach you how presented technologies work. I do not explain configuration examples but if you do not feel confident to perform troubleshooting effectively, the book is for you.

Contents

1 Preface 10
2 Traffic flow 12
    2.1 Diagnose session 12
    2.2 Reverse Path Forwarding 26
    2.3 Firewall Policy NAT 26
        2.3.1 Source NAT 27
        2.3.2 Destination NAT 32
        2.3.3 NAT configuration errors 35
    2.4 Central NAT 37
        2.4.1 Source NAT 37
        2.4.2 Destination NAT 38
    2.5 Policy Lookup 41
3 Traffic Inspection 42
    3.1 Inspection mode 42
    3.2 Web Filtering 46
    3.3 Antivirus 50
        3.3.1 Flow-based inspection mode 50
        3.3.2 Proxy-based inspection mode 52
    3.4 IPS 54
4 VPN 57
    4.1 IPsec 57
        4.1.1 Example #1 57
        4.1.2 Example #2 – pre-share secret mismatch 69
        4.1.3 Example #3 – phase1 mismatch settings (authentication, encryption) 70
        4.1.4 Example #4 – phase2 mismatch settings (selectors) 74
        4.1.5 Example #5 – mismatch IKE mode (aggressive vs main mode) 77

- 4.1.6 Example #6 – mismatch IKE versions (IKEv1 vs IKEv2) 79
- 4.2 SSL-VPN 81
  - 4.2.1 Example #1 – web-based mode 81
  - 4.2.2 Example #2 – tunnel-based mode 83
  - 4.2.3 Example #3 – invalid user 85
  - 4.2.4 Example #4 – user not permitted to web-based mode 86
  - 4.2.5 Example #5 – user not permitted to tunnel mode 86
- 5 Routing 88
  - 5.1 Static 88
    - 5.1.1 Policy Base Routing 92
    - 5.1.2 Link Health Monitor 93
  - 5.2 OSPF 95
  - 5.3 BGP 111
- 6 High Availability 122
  - 6.1 FortiGate Clustering Protocol (FGCP) 122
  - 6.2 Virtual Router Routing Protocol (VRRP) 126
- 7 Load Balancing 130
- 8 Admin access 136
  - 8.1 Local-in Policy 136
  - 8.2 Trusted Source 138
  - 8.3 HTTPS access vs SSL-VPN 138
- 9 Hardware (CPU, memory, disk, flash) 139
  - 9.1 Hardware status 139
  - 9.2 Network Interface Card 140
  - 9.3 Network Processor 144
  - 9.4 Transceiver 146
  - 9.5 System performance 147

	9.6	Sys top	149
	9.7	Flash and disk	151
10		Other - uncategorized	154
	10.1	ARP	154
	10.2	LAG	155
	10.3	Configuration Management Database (CMDB)	158
	10.4	Grep	158
	10.5	Crashlog	159
	10.6	TAC	160
11		Index	162

1 Preface

Troubleshooting, next to network design and implementation, is one of the most demanding skill in computer network industry. One of the differences between them is time expected to complete the task. In troubleshooting you always work under time pressure. Everyone wants to know root cause and fix the incident as soon as possible. In my 20+ year career, I participated in hundreds of troubleshooting calls and I learnt the following principals regarding what you should know before you start:

- what is the problem?
- understand the network design/network diagram
- understand common protocols/applications
- well-structured troubleshooting approach
- troubleshooting commands

The first seems to be obvious, but believe me, after 10 hours on call with many people talking about their views on the problem, you can get lost. Do not be afraid to ask questions, until you have a good overview of the problem. Today's networks are complex. Applications are complex too. We, network/security engineers, are not application or database specialists. We need to know all symptoms, provided in the format: "no access between source and destination", IP addresses, transport protocol, ports, etc.

The second point on the list is the network design. By this one, I mean understanding of all components, or at least those ones, which are relevant to the traffic flow. I know that sometimes we do not have such privilege to know the network well before the incident appears. We can be engaged to join a bridge to solve an issue in totally foreign environment. That is fine, just spend more time on understanding the traffic flow.

The first two items on the list can be learnt or asked during the troubleshooting. At the beginning of the call it is totally fine to spend some time to gather all the details needed. About the next three, you should know before the problem appears. When you understand the protocols, and what should be checked first, more time can be spent on effective investigation. When you do not understand the protocol or the framework of protocols, such as IPsec, probably you jump from one place to another without any structured approach. Once you understand all protocols/applications and the troubleshooting approach, then it will just become obvious. For example, understanding IPsec phases, and their variations (i.e.: phase 1 aggressive vs. main mode), you know that it makes more sense to verify the phase1 first. If it fails, there is no way to negotiate IPsec SAs. If the Internet connection is failing every couple of minutes, tearing down the VPN tunnel, it does not make sense to test the application, which is running on top of the VPN. If something does not work make sure the underlying service is fine: Internet connection -> VPN phase1 -> VPN phase2 -> connectivity between hosts, etc. There are couple of troubleshooting methods you can follow (from bottom layer up, from the top down, follow the path, etc.), but I prefer to take final decision once I gather all information about the incident I am working on.

The last one is understanding the troubleshooting commands for a specific device. When the platform is new for you, instead of thinking about the problem, you spend most of the time on guessing or searching how to get the information from the system. It is very ineffective approach and it should be avoided. There is no need to remember all commands. It is fine to have them handy. Today, with so many systems with different syntax we must support, I do not even try to remember all commands. For this reason, I decided to write this book to help you with it. I hope you find the information presented here useful during your troubleshooting. Good luck!

2 Traffic flow

The most common problem in the network is lack of connectivity between two hosts. Probably you heard it many times: "it doesn't work" or "I don't have access to …". Sometimes it is caused by a node or link failure, and sometimes because devices, like firewalls, block the connection intentionally. It could be your task to find it out. On FortiGate there are many tools, which can help you during the investigation. In the next few chapters I will show you 'how' and 'when' to use them.

2.1 Diagnose session

Before we start the troubleshooting, you should learn how to verify if the traffic is allowed or denied. There are couple of methods:

a) Verify the session table – simple view

Example 2.1

```
forti (test) # get system session list
PROTO   EXPIRE  SOURCE                  SOURCE-NAT      DESTINATION             DESTINATION-NAT
tcp     3559    10.0.48.139:55506  -                    192.168.40.20:27017 -
udp     132     172.16.52.11:36094 -                    172.16.161.22:53   -
tcp     4       192.168.134.152:60655 -                 10.2.3.45:135      -
udp     118     192.168.134.87:52408 -                  10.2.3.20:53       -
tcp     9       172.16.105.252:3178 -                   192.168.2.188:443  -
```

The above session list is the confirmation that the traffic is allowed by the firewall. Let's analyze the output:

- PROTO is a protocol, and in the above example you can see TCP and UDP sessions.

- EXPIRE, this is TTL session timer (counting down). The default value for TCP is 3600 seconds.
- SOURCE - in the third column, you can see source IP along with the source port.
- SOURCE-NAT - there is no source NAT configured, so we do not see any value in the column.
- DESTINATION - in the fifth column you see the destination IP and the port number.
- DESTINATION-NAT - there is no destination NAT set for these sessions.

I explain source and destination NAT later in this chapter.

In production the list of sessions can be very long. There is no filter built-in the command, but you can use **grep** to filter out the list:

Example 2.2

```
forti (test) # get system session list | grep tcp
```

b) Verify the session table – detailed view

There is a version of the **session list** command, with much more details. I marked the most important information in the below output.

Example 2.3

```
forti (test) # diagnose sys session list


session info: proto=6 proto_state=05 duration=2 expire=0 timeout=3600 flags=00000000 sockflag=00000000 sockport=0 av_idx=0 use=5

origin-shaper=

reply-shaper=

per_ip_shaper=

ha_id=0 policy_dir=0 tunnel=/ vlan_cos=0/255

state=log may_dirty npu synced f00
```

```
statistic(bytes/packets/allow_err): org=1269/16/1 reply=29870/25/1 tuples=2
tx speed(Bps/kbps): 628/5 rx speed(Bps/kbps): 14787/118
orgin->sink: org pre->post, reply pre->post dev=61->101/101->61 gwy=10.24.2.17/10.11.2.10
hook=pre dir=org act=noop 10.54.3.16:35563->10.8.1.141:80(0.0.0.0:0)
hook=post dir=reply act=noop 10.8.1.141:80->10.54.3.16:35563(0.0.0.0:0)
pos/(before,after) 0/(0,0), 0/(0,0)
misc=0 policy_id=211 auth_info=0 chk_client_info=0 vd=1
serial=0c034224 tos=ff/ff app_list=0 app=0 url_cat=0
dd_type=0 dd_mode=0
npu_state=0x000c00
npu info: flag=0x00/0x00, offload=0/0, ips_offload=0/0, epid=147/146, ipid=146/147,
vlan=0x0036/0x0da2
vlifid=146/147, vtag_in=0x0036/0x0da2 in_npu=1/1, out_npu=1/1, fwd_en=0/0, qid=0/0
no_ofld_reason:
ofld_fail_reason(kernel, drv): not-established/not-established, none(0)/none(0)
npu_state_err=04/04
```

Let's analyze what we can see in the output:

- proto –
    - TCP = 6
    - UDP = 17
- proto_state –
    - the first digit:
        - 0 – flow-based inspection
        - 1 – proxy-based inspection
    - the second digit:
        - 1 – established
        - 2 – syn sent
        - 3 – syn + syn/ack sent
        - 4 - fin wait
        - 5 – time wait
        - 6 – close

- - - 7 – close wait
    - 8 last ACK
    - 9 - listen
  - state –
    - log – logged session
    - local – connection from or to the FortiGate
    - may _dirty – initial evaluation of the session
    - npu – can be offloaded to NPU ASIC
    - npd – session cannot be offloaded for the ASIC
    - synced – information the session is synced with HA cluster member
  - gwy –
    - first IP – IP gateway for the first packet
    - second IP – IP gateway for reply packet
  - dir – direction: org and reply plus pair of IP for each flow – there is no NAT (0.0.0.0:0)
  - policy_id – the firewall policy which accepts the traffic

There is a way to filter out the list of the sessions. In the below output there are all available options:

Example 2.4

```
forti (test) # diagnose sys session filter ?
vd              Index of virtual domain. -1 matches all.
sintf           Source interface.
dintf           Destination interface.
src             Source IP address.
nsrc            NAT'd source ip address
dst             Destination IP address.
proto           Protocol number.
sport           Source port.
nport           NAT'd source port
dport           Destination port.
```

policy	Policy ID.
expire	expire
duration	duration
proto-state	Protocol state.
session-state1	Session state1.
session-state2	Session state2.
ext-src	Add a source address to the extended match list.
ext-dst	Add a destination address to the extended match list.
ext-src-negate	Add a source address to the negated extended match list.
ext-dst-negate	Add a destination address to the negated extended match list.
clear	Clear session filter.
negate	Inverse filter.

```
forti (test) #
```

When the session you are looking for is not on the list, you can check packets arriving on the interface. There are two commands available. The first one, packet capture, shows you ingress and egress packets. This is the best way to spot missing reply from the server (no SYN/ACK). In such case there is entry in the session table as the session is not established. Remember, the ingress packet must be permitted first by the firewall policy.

c) Perform the packet capture

Example 2.5

```
forti (test) # diagnose sniffer packet any 'host 10.16.2.16' 4 10 a
interfaces=[any]
filters=[host 10.16.2.16]
2019-10-15 18:24:44.957356 vlan5 in 10.16.2.16.36558 -> 172.16.4.12.80: syn 2099736475
2019-10-15 18:24:44.957373 vlan3 out 10.16.2.16.36558 -> 172.16.4.12.80: syn 2099736475
```

```
2019-10-15 18:24:44.957374 port4 out 10.16.2.16.36558 -> 172.16.4.12.80: syn 2099736475
2019-10-15 18:24:44.957509 vlan3 in 172.16.4.12.80 -> 10.16.2.16.36558: syn 1002812911 ack 2099736476
2019-10-15 18:24:44.957522 vlan5 out 172.16.4.12.80 -> 10.16.2.16.36558: syn 1002812911 ack 2099736476
2019-10-15 18:24:44.957523 port3 out 172.16.4.12.80 -> 10.16.2.16.36558: syn 1002812911 ack 2099736476
2019-10-15 18:24:44.957849 vlan5 in 10.16.2.16.36558 -> 172.16.4.12.80: ack 1002812912
2019-10-15 18:24:44.957857 vlan3 out 10.16.2.16.36558 -> 172.16.4.12.80: ack 1002812912
2019-10-15 18:24:44.957858 port4 out 10.16.2.16.36558 -> 172.16.4.12.80: ack 1002812912
```

The command **diagnose sniffer packet** has many parameters:

- interface – you can specify a physical or VLAN interface or use keyword 'any'
- filter - on the above example you can see filter for specific IP but you can use more advanced expressions: '**tcp and port 443 and host 1.2.3.4 and (4.4.4.1 or 8.8.8.8)**', '**src net 10.1.10.0/24**' or just 'none'
- verbose – I used verbose level '4' to see interfaces but there are more options here and you will see more examples in this chapter:
    - 1: print header of the packets
    - 2: print header and data from IP of the packets
    - 3: print header and data from ethernet of the packets (if available)
    - 4: print header of packets with interface name
    - 5: print header and data from IP of the packets with the interface name
    - 6: print header and data from ethernet of the packets (if available) with intf name
- count – number of packets you want capture (optional)
- timestamp - the parameter is also optional, and you can set: a – absolute UTC, l – local, or leave it empty and it will show time from the start of the sniffing

Remember when 'any' interface is set, you can see the same packet more times. It depends on the interface configuration. In our example the SYN packet is seen three times:

- vlan5 in
- vlan3 out

- port4 out

What does it mean? Packet arrives on vlan5 interface, then, once permitted, it is sent out via vlan3 interface. You can see also port4 because vlan3 is a sub-interface of port4. There is no incoming traffic on the physical interface.

The second packet SYN/ACK is the returning packet:

- vlan3 in
- vlan5 out
- port3 out

The packet appears three times as well, because vlan5 is a sub-interface of port3.

Make sure, not to set physical interface in the filter when you use VLANs as interfaces without IP cannot be used. In the below example you can see the error message:

Example 2.6

```
forti (test) # diagnose sniffer packet port3 'host 10.16.2.16' 4 10 a
interfaces=[port3]
filters=[host 10.16.2.16]
pcap_lookupnet: port3: no IPv4 address assigned
```

The example 2.7 shows the output only for one interface vlan5, and the same packet appears just once.

Example 2.7

```
forti (test) # diagnose sniffer packet vlan5 'host 10.16.2.16' 4 10 a
interfaces=[vlan5]
filters=[host 10.16.2.16]
2019-10-15 18:29:49.238673 vlan5 -- 10.16.2.16.11546 -> 172.16.4.12.80: syn 4006991971
2019-10-15 18:29:49.238815 vlan5 -- 172.16.4.12.80 -> 10.16.2.16.11546: syn 1397932339 ack 4006991972
2019-10-15 18:29:49.239159 vlan5 -- 10.16.2.16.11546 -> 172.16.4.12.80: ack 1397932340
```

In the example 2.8 you can see filter set for vlan3, and in the output there is only one copy of the packet.

Example 2.8

```
forti (test) # diagnose sniffer packet vlan3 'host 10.16.2.16' 4 10 a
interfaces=[vlan3]
filters=[host 10.16.2.16]
2019-10-15 18:30:26.020013 vlan3 -- 10.16.2.16.28183 -> 172.16.4.12.80: syn 912710974
2019-10-15 18:30:26.020108 vlan3 -- 172.16.4.12.80 -> 10.16.2.16.28183: syn 80195551 ack 912710975
2019-10-15 18:30:26.020441 vlan3 -- 10.16.2.16.28183 -> 172.16.4.12.80: ack 80195552
```

When there is no need to see the interface name for every packet, you can set verbose 1. It shows the same level of information (except the interface name):

Example 2.9

```
forti (test) # diagnose sniffer packet vlan5 'host 10.16.2.16' 1 10 a
interfaces=[vlan5]
filters=[host 10.16.2.16]
2019-10-15 18:30:59.747995 10.16.2.16.46331 -> 172.16.4.10.80: syn 4101630887
2019-10-15 18:30:59.748157 172.16.4.10.80 -> 10.16.2.16.46331: syn 3607294891 ack 4101630888
2019-10-15 18:30:59.748494 10.16.2.16.46331 -> 172.16.4.10.80: psh 4101632323 ack 3607294892
2019-10-15 18:30:59.748507 10.16.2.16.46331 -> 172.16.4.10.80: ack 3607294892
2019-10-15 18:30:59.748513 10.16.2.16.46331 -> 172.16.4.10.80: 4101630888 ack 3607294892
```

When you need to look at IP packet data, you can select verbosity 2:

Example 2.10

```
forti (test) # diagnose sniffer packet vlan5 'host 10.16.2.16' 2 3 a
interfaces=[vlan5]
filters=[host 10.16.2.16]
2019-10-15 18:31:38.291860 10.16.2.16.60602 -> 172.16.4.12.80: syn 1049815025
0x0000   4500 003c b204 4000 fb06 14e3 ac1c 3010      E..<..@.......0.
0x0010   ac1a 308d ecba 0050 3e92 e7f1 0000 0000      ..0....P>.......
0x0020   a002 111c 00a2 0000 0204 05b4 0101 080a      ................
0x0030   d0b0 9c37 0000 0000 0402 0000               ...7........


2019-10-15 18:31:38.291969 172.16.4.12.80 -> 10.16.2.16.60602: syn 1661756760 ack 1049815026
0x0000   4500 0038 0000 4000 3e06 83ec ac1a 308d      E..8..@.>.....0.
0x0010   ac1c 3010 0050 ecba 630c 6558 3e92 e7f2      ..0..P..c.eX>...
0x0020   9012 7120 7ff3 0000 0204 05b4 0402 080a      ..q.............
0x0030   d7a1 9197 d0b0 9c37                          .......7


2019-10-15 18:31:38.292275 10.16.2.16.60602 -> 172.16.4.12.80: ack 1661756761
0x0000   4500 0034 b207 4000 fb06 14e8 ac1c 3010      E..4..@.......0.
0x0010   ac1a 308d ecba 0050 3e92 e7f2 630c 6559      ..0....P>...c.eY
0x0020   8010 111c fab4 0000 0101 080a d0b0 9c38      ...............8
0x0030   d7a1 9197                                    ....
```

Verbosity 5 includes the same details as verbosity 1, but it displays interface names. For more details like ethernet data, you can select verbosity 3 or 6.

Remember, when the traffic is dropped by the firewall, there will be no traffic in the packet capture. In that case, you need **debug flow** command, which is explained below.

    d) Check the debug flow

Debug flow has more visibility into system, and it can report every packet which arrives on the interface. It will show how the packet is processed and what is the final decision: allow or drop. The command has more parameters, and you set them as separate commands. In the below example, the filter is set for source and destination IP addresses. The last parameter 100 means how many packets I want to see.

Example 2.11

```
diagnose debug reset     <- it's a good practice to reset all debugs before you start new one
diagnose debug flow filter clear  <- it's a good practice to clear filters before you set new

diagnose debug flow filter saddr 10.16.2.16
diagnose debug flow filter daddr 172.16.4.10
diagnose debug flow show function-name enable
diagnose debug flow trace start 100

diagnose debug enable
```

It is very important to disable debug and reset all settings/filters once finished. I recommend starting the debug with a reset, to make sure not to use filters you have set earlier.

Example 2.12

```
diagnose debug reset
diagnose debug disable
```

The most important parameter is the filter. You do not want to see all packets. I think the filter options are self-explanatory:

Example 2.13

```
forti (test) # diagnose debug flow filter
clear    Clear filter.
vd       Index of virtual domain.
proto    Protocol number.
addr     IP address.
saddr    Source IP address.
daddr    Destination IP address.
port     port
sport    Source port.
dport    Destination port.
negate   Inverse filter.

forti (test) #
```

Once we set proper filters, we will get a lot of useful information. I recommend logging the output into a file for further analysis. You will not be able to analyze every packet looking at the console.

In the below example you can spot the first packet of the new session. There are couple of interesting details highlighted in the below output.

Example 2.14

```
id=20085 trace_id=217 func=print_pkt_detail line=5375 msg="vd-test received a packet(proto=6, 10.16.2.16:22167->172.16.4.10:80) from vlan5. flag [S], seq 4283788036, ack 0, win 4380"

id=20085 trace_id=217 func=init_ip_session_common line=5534 msg="allocate a new session-0c22ee5d"

id=20085 trace_id=217 func=vf_ip_route_input_common line=2574 msg="find a route: flag=00000000 gw-192.168.6.9 via vlan3"

id=20085 trace_id=217 func=fw_forward_handler line=743 msg="Allowed by Policy-16:"
```

Let's analyze all highlighted details:

- msg – vd-test received a packet – name of VDOM where the packet arrived, you can see root in the device without VDOMs
- proto=6 – TCP
- source and destination IPs (+ports)
- from vlan5 – incoming interface
- flag [S] – TCP SYN flag
- msg="allocate a new session…" – it means there was no existing session for that packet/flow and FortiGate allocated a new one
- msg="find a route:" – before FortiGate starts firewall policy lookup, an exit interface is required. FortiGate checks routing table twice: for the first initiated and first reply packets.
- gw-192.168.6.9 via vlan3 – the gateway and exit interface found during the route lookup operation
- msg="Allowed by Policy-16" – once all details are known (source and destination IP address, ingress and egress interfaces, service, port, etc.), FortiGate can perform policy lookup. In this case the firewall policy with ID 16 matches, and the action is 'allowed'.

The above packet was the initial one in the TCP communication. The second is the reply packet – SYN/ACK. Let's analyze what we see here:

Example 2.15

```
id=20085 trace_id=218 func=print_pkt_detail line=5375 msg="vd-test received a packet(proto=6, 172.16.4.10:80->10.16.2.16:22167) from vlan3. flag [S.], seq 3882227979, ack 4283788037, win 28960"

id=20085 trace_id=218 func=resolve_ip_tuple_fast line=5450 msg="Find an existing session, id-0c22ee5d, reply direction"

id=20085 trace_id=218 func=vf_ip_route_input_common line=2574 msg="find a route: flag=00000000 gw-192.168.4.3 via vlan5"

id=20085 trace_id=218 func=npu_handle_session44 line=1096 msg="Trying to offloading session from vlan3 to vlan5, skb.npu_flag=00000400 ses.state=04010204 ses.npu_state=0x00000000"

id=20085 trace_id=218 func=ip_session_install_npu_session line=351 msg="npu session installation succeeded"
```

- msg – vd-test received a packet – name of VDOM where the packet arrived
- proto=6 – TCP
- source and destination IPs (+ports) – reply packet from the server
- from vlan3 – incoming interface for the reply packet
- flag [S.] – TCP SYN/ACK flag
- msg="Find an existing session..." – it means the existing session was found and matched for the returning packet/flow. You can also see the session ID
- msg="find a route:" – this the second time when FortiGate verifies routing, for the first reply packet
- gw-192.168.4.3 via vlan5 – the gateway and exit interface found during the route lookup operation
- msg="Trying to offloading session from vlan3 to vlan5,..." – FortiGate attempts to offload the session to NPU (ASIC Network Processor Unit)
- msg="npu session installation succeeded" – the confirmation that was successfully off-loaded to NPU

You saw two packets in the initial 3-way TCP handshake. Below is the final one:

Example 2.16

```
id=20085 trace_id=219 func=print_pkt_detail line=5375 msg="vd-test received a packet(proto=6, 10.16.2.16:22167->172.16.4.10:80) from vlan5. flag [.], seq 4283788037, ack 3882227980, win 4380"

id=20085 trace_id=219 func=resolve_ip_tuple_fast line=5450 msg="Find an existing session, id-0c22ee5d, original direction"

id=20085 trace_id=219 func=npu_handle_session44 line=1096 msg="Trying to offloading session from vlan5 to vlan3, skb.npu_flag=00000400 ses.state=04010204 ses.npu_state=0x00000800"

id=20085 trace_id=219 func=ip_session_install_npu_session line=351 msg="npu session installation succeeded"
```

- msg – vd-test received a packet – name of VDOM where the packet arrived
- proto=6 – TCP
- source and destination IPs (+ports) –packet from the initiator to the server

- from vlan5 – incoming interface for the 3rd packet
- flag [.] – TCP ACK flag
- msg="Find an existing session..." –the existing session was found and matched for the packet/flow
- msg="Trying to offloading session from vlan5 to vlan3,..." – attempts to offload the session to NPU (ASIC Network Processor Unit)
- msg="npu session installation succeeded" – the confirmation the was successfully off-loaded to NPU

All the above examples present the accepted packets. Now it is time to look at an example of denied traffic:

Example 2.17

```
diagnose debug flow filter addr 10.12.5.16
diagnose debug flow show function-name enable
diagnose debug flow trace start 10
diagnose debug enable
```

In the below example there is a message 'Denied by forward policy check (policy O)'. In this case FortiGate must perform route lookup before it checks firewall polices (to know the exit interface):

Example 2.18

```
id=20085 trace_id=2440 func=print_pkt_detail line=5347 msg="vd-test received a packet(proto=6, 10.12.5.16:56016->8.8.8.8:443) from vlan25. flag [S], seq 1372470198, ack 0, win 8192"

id=20085 trace_id=2440 func=init_ip_session_common line=5506 msg="allocate a new session-319f254e"

id=20085 trace_id=2440 func=vf_ip_route_input_common line=2574 msg="find a route: flag=00000000 gw-192.168.1.1 via vlan4"

id=20085 trace_id=2440 func=fw_forward_handler line=591 msg="Denied by forward policy check (policy 0)"
```

Policy ID 0 is the implicit deny policy. This is the last, built-in, policy in the firewall policy table. There will be more examples of denied packets later in this chapter.

2.2 Reverse Path Forwarding

RPF is a control mechanism to drop packets with spoofed source IP address. It permits packets with a source IP address, for which FortiGate knows about, which in network terminology means that has a matching entry in its routing table. What is also important, the routing entry must have the same outgoing interface as incoming interface on which the packets arrived. For example, you receive a packet with an IP source 10.1.1.1 on a port3. FortiGate verifies its routing table and permits the packet only when in the routing table there is a matching entry for that IP address that has port3 as the outgoing interface. There are two variations of the RPF: loose (or feasible) and strict mode. The second one checks if the path via the incoming interface of the packet, is the best route.

Diagnose debug flow can show you when the packet is dropped due to the RPF checks:

Example 2.19

```
id=20085 trace_id=200 func=print_pkt_detail line=5497 msg="vd-root:0 received a packet(proto=6, 211.104.57.57:1704->8.8.8.8:0) from port5. flag [S], seq 1845508360, ack 60760960, win 512"

id=20085 trace_id=200 func=init_ip_session_common line=5657 msg="allocate a new session-000008ba"

id=20085 trace_id=200 func=ip_route_input_slow line=2249 msg="reverse path check fail, drop"

id=20085 trace_id=200 func=ip_session_handle_no_dst line=5733 msg="trace"
```

2.3 Firewall Policy NAT

FortiGate in NAT operation mode (L3) can work in Firewall Policy NAT (default) or Central NAT. In the default settings you set source and destination NAT for each firewall policy. From the troubleshooting perspective there is no difference which method is set. The packet can be properly NAT-ed or not. The only difference is in the order, how the packet is processed.

2.3.1 Source NAT

For each firewall policy you can enable source NAT and choose between NAT-ing on the outgoing interface or to one of the IP addresses specified in the SNAT pool. The best method to verify if the SNAT is performed is to check **get system session list** and **diagnose debug flow**, which were described above.

In the below example there is traffic which is SNAT-ed on the exit interface of the firewall (column SOURCE-NAT):

Example 2.20

```
forti # get system session list
PROTO   EXPIRE  SOURCE                SOURCE-NAT          DESTINATION         DESTINATION-NAT
tcp     3424    192.168.11.100:49682  172.16.1.1:49682    172.217.14.206:80   -
```

and to verify how the NAT is performed check **diagnose debug flow** output:

Example 2.21

```
diagnose debug reset
diagnose debug flow filter addr 172.217.14.206
diagnose debug flow show function-name enable
diagnose debug flow trace start 100
diagnose debug enable
```

When the first packet arrives, FortiGate will perform the following:

- allocates a new session

- performs route lookup to identify the exit interface
- performs firewall policy lookup to verify if the traffic is allowed or not, and if SNAT is enabled

In the below example, you can see all these steps, including SNAT for the initial TCP communication (TCP with flag SYN):

Example 2.22

```
func=print_pkt_detail line=5497 msg="vd-root:0 received a packet(proto=6,
192.168.11.100:49682->172.217.14.206:80) from port5. flag [S], seq 966157991, ack 0, win
8192"

id=20085 trace_id=56 func=init_ip_session_common line=5657 msg="allocate a new session-
000002de"

id=20085 trace_id=56 func=vf_ip_route_input_common line=2591 msg="find a route:
flag=04000000 gw-172.16.1.254 via port2"

id=20085 trace_id=56 func=fw_forward_handler line=751 msg="Allowed by Policy-101: SNAT"

id=20085 trace_id=56 func=__ip_session_run_tuple line=3328 msg="SNAT 192.168.11.100-
>172.16.1.1:49682"
```

The reply packet from the server is sent to NAT-ed IP (172.16.1.1). FortiGate must reverse the SNAT operation, and you can see it here (as DNAT):

Example 2.23

```
id=20085 trace_id=57 func=print_pkt_detail line=5497 msg="vd-root:0 received a
packet(proto=6, 172.217.14.206:80->172.16.1.1:49682) from port2. flag [S.], seq 972739247,
ack 966157992, win 60720"

id=20085 trace_id=57 func=resolve_ip_tuple_fast line=5572 msg="Find an existing session, id-
000002de, reply direction"

id=20085 trace_id=57 func=__ip_session_run_tuple line=3342 msg="DNAT 172.16.1.1:49682-
>192.168.11.100:49682"

id=20085 trace_id=57 func=vf_ip_route_input_common line=2591 msg="find a route:
flag=00000000 gw-192.168.11.100 via port5"
```

As explained in the previous chapter, from the initial packet and the first reply from the server, FortiGate must find a route (and the exit interface). You do not see the same in the final TCP ACK:

Example 2.24

```
id=20085 trace_id=58 func=print_pkt_detail line=5497 msg="vd-root:0 received a packet(proto=6, 192.168.11.100:49682->172.217.14.206:80) from port5. flag [.], seq 966157992, ack 972739248, win 258"

id=20085 trace_id=58 func=resolve_ip_tuple_fast line=5572 msg="Find an existing session, id-000002de, original direction"

id=20085 trace_id=58 func=ipv4_fast_cb line=53 msg="enter fast path"

id=20085 trace_id=58 func=ip_session_run_all_tuple line=6738 msg="SNAT 192.168.11.100->172.16.1.1:49682"
```

When you have more users, you may need a pool of IP addresses to perform the SNAT. Let's assume we have the following IP pool configured:

Example 2.25

```
forti # diagnose firewall ippool-all stats
vdom:root owns 1 ippool(s)
name: test-IP-pool
type: overload
startip: 172.16.1.100
endip: 172.16.1.101
total ses: 25
tcp ses: 25
udp ses: 0
other ses: 0
```

From the session perspective, there is no difference between sessions with SNAT on the interface or SNAT IP picked from the IP pool:

Example 2.26

```
forti # get system session list
PROTO   EXPIRE  SOURCE                 SOURCE-NAT            DESTINATION          DESTINATION-NAT
tcp     3434    192.168.11.100:50049   172.16.1.101:50049    172.217.14.206:80    -
```

Even from the below output, you can't see, that the IP is allocated from the IP pool:

Example 2.27

```
id=20085 trace_id=91 func=print_pkt_detail line=5497 msg="vd-root:0 received a
packet(proto=6, 192.168.11.100:50049->172.217.14.206:80) from port5. flag [S], seq
3173586349, ack 0, win 8192"

id=20085 trace_id=91 func=init_ip_session_common line=5657 msg="allocate a new session-
0000063c"

id=20085 trace_id=91 func=vf_ip_route_input_common line=2591 msg="find a route:
flag=04000000 gw-172.16.1.254 via port2"

id=20085 trace_id=91 func=fw_forward_handler line=751 msg="Allowed by Policy-101: SNAT"

id=20085 trace_id=91 func=__ip_session_run_tuple line=3328 msg="SNAT 192.168.11.100-
>172.16.1.101:50049"
```

The rest of the packets are processed as it was in the previous example:

Example 2.28

```
id=20085 trace_id=92 func=print_pkt_detail line=5497 msg="vd-root:0 received a
packet(proto=6, 172.217.14.206:80->172.16.1.101:50049) from port2. flag [S.], seq
2901848098, ack 3173586350, win 60720"

id=20085 trace_id=92 func=resolve_ip_tuple_fast line=5572 msg="Find an existing session, id-
0000063c, reply direction"

id=20085 trace_id=92 func=__ip_session_run_tuple line=3342 msg="DNAT 172.16.1.101:50049-
>192.168.11.100:50049"
```

```
id=20085 trace_id=92 func=vf_ip_route_input_common line=2591 msg="find a route:
flag=00000000 gw-192.168.11.100 via port5"
```

And the final TCP 3-way handshake – TCP ACK:

Example 2.29

```
id=20085 trace_id=93 func=print_pkt_detail line=5497 msg="vd-root:0 received a
packet(proto=6, 192.168.11.100:50049->172.217.14.206:80) from port5. flag [.], seq
3173586350, ack 2901848099, win 258"

id=20085 trace_id=93 func=resolve_ip_tuple_fast line=5572 msg="Find an existing session, id-
0000063c, original direction"

id=20085 trace_id=93 func=ipv4_fast_cb line=53 msg="enter fast path"

id=20085 trace_id=93 func=ip_session_run_all_tuple line=6738 msg="SNAT 192.168.11.100-
>172.16.1.101:50049"
```

We analyzed examples for traffic which was permitted without any issues. How the **diagnose debug flow** output may look like when something goes wrong? Assume we forgot to enable SNAT in the firewall policy ID 101. You see three attempts to establish the connection. The same TCP SYN packet is sent but there is no response from the server. There is no information about SNAT action, which means that the FortiGate sends the packets with the original IP address. If the next device does not have that IP/subnet in the routing table, the packet is dropped.

Example 2.30

```
id=20085 trace_id=82 func=print_pkt_detail line=5497 msg="vd-root:0 received a
packet(proto=6, 192.168.11.100:49877->172.217.14.206:80) from port5. flag [S], seq
3221646088, ack 0, win 8192"

id=20085 trace_id=82 func=init_ip_session_common line=5657 msg="allocate a new session-
000004c2"

id=20085 trace_id=82 func=vf_ip_route_input_common line=2591 msg="find a route:
flag=04000000 gw-172.16.1.254 via port2"

id=20085 trace_id=82 func=fw_forward_handler line=751 msg="Allowed by Policy-101:"
```

```
id=20085 trace_id=83 func=print_pkt_detail line=5497 msg="vd-root:0 received a
packet(proto=6, 192.168.11.100:49877->172.217.14.206:80) from port5. flag [S], seq
3221646088, ack 0, win 8192"

id=20085 trace_id=83 func=resolve_ip_tuple_fast line=5572 msg="Find an existing session, id-
000004c2, original direction"

id=20085 trace_id=83 func=ipv4_fast_cb line=53 msg="enter fast path"


id=20085 trace_id=84 func=print_pkt_detail line=5497 msg="vd-root:0 received a
packet(proto=6, 192.168.11.100:49877->172.217.14.206:80) from port5. flag [S], seq
3221646088, ack 0, win 8192"

id=20085 trace_id=84 func=resolve_ip_tuple_fast line=5572 msg="Find an existing session, id-
000004c2, original direction"

id=20085 trace_id=84 func=ipv4_fast_cb line=53 msg="enter fast path"
```

2.3.2 Destination NAT

In Firewall Policy NAT the destination NAT (DNAT) is implemented in two steps. First, you need a VIP object in which you define mapping between real and mapped IP addresses. On FortiGate you can do one-to-one (static) mapping or one-to-many IPs (load balancing/server load balancing). I will explain the concept in the 'Load Balancing' chapter. In next step, you add the VIP object to the destination field in the firewall policy window. NAT details can be verified by checking the session list:

Example 2.31

```
forti # get system session list
PROTO   EXPIRE  SOURCE          SOURCE-NAT      DESTINATION     DESTINATION-NAT
icmp    52      10.5.5.1:256    -               10.7.7.20:8     192.168.11.100:256
```

This is the definition of the VIP:

Example 2.32

```
forti # sh firewall vip
config firewall vip
    edit "test-VIP-object"
        ...
        set extip 10.7.7.20 <- the real IP
        set extintf "any"
        set mappedip "192.168.11.100"
    next
end
```

When you experience any issue with the DNAT, use **diagnose debug flow** command, and verify what is the destination IP in the packet, before and after NAT operation.

In the below example ICMP packet (proto=1) echo request (type=8, code=0) is sent from host 10.5.5.1 to VIP 10.7.7.20. This is the order of operations on the FortiGate:

- allocates a new session
- finds a VIP object with matching destination IP (VIP-192.168.11.100)
- performs DNAT, by translating VIP to the real IP address
- searches a route for the real destination IP address, and identify an outgoing interface
- checks if there is any matching firewall policy

Example 2.33

```
id=20085 trace_id=203 func=print_pkt_detail line=5497 msg="vd-root:0 received a packet(proto=1, 10.5.5.1:0->10.7.7.20:2048) from port2. type=8, code=0, id=0, seq=0."

id=20085 trace_id=203 func=init_ip_session_common line=5657 msg="allocate a new session-00000922"

id=20085 trace_id=203 func=fw_pre_route_handler line=182 msg="VIP-192.168.11.100:8, outdev-unkown"

id=20085 trace_id=203 func=__ip_session_run_tuple line=3342 msg="DNAT 10.7.7.20:8->192.168.11.100:8"
```

```
id=20085 trace_id=203 func=vf_ip_route_input_common line=2591 msg="find a route:
flag=00000000 gw-192.168.11.100 via port5"

id=20085 trace_id=203 func=fw_forward_handler line=751 msg="Allowed by Policy-2:"
```

The return packet, echo reply (type=0, code=0) is sent back to the host 10.5.5.1. FortiGate needs to modify the real source IP in the reply to the mapped one, according to the VIP definition. SNAT is performed, which is de facto reverse of the DNAT operation, done a step earlier.

Example 2.34

```
id=20085 trace_id=204 func=print_pkt_detail line=5497 msg="vd-root:0 received a
packet(proto=1, 192.168.11.100:8->10.5.5.1:0) from port5. type=0, code=0, id=8, seq=0."

id=20085 trace_id=204 func=resolve_ip_tuple_fast line=5572 msg="Find an existing session,
id-00000922, reply direction"

id=20085 trace_id=204 func=vf_ip_route_input_common line=2591 msg="find a route:
flag=04000000 gw-10.5.5.254 via port2"

id=20085 trace_id=204 func=__ip_session_run_tuple line=3328 msg="SNAT 192.168.11.100-
>10.7.7.20:0"
```

The next ICMP echo request can be matched on the existing session. FortiGate does not check the routing table and firewall policies. DNAT operation is performed as per log entry in the last line:

Example 2.35

```
id=20085 trace_id=205 func=print_pkt_detail line=5497 msg="vd-root:0 received a
packet(proto=1, 10.5.5.1:0->10.7.7.20:2048) from port2. type=8, code=0, id=0, seq=1."

id=20085 trace_id=205 func=resolve_ip_tuple_fast line=5572 msg="Find an existing session,
id-00000922, original direction"

id=20085 trace_id=205 func=ipv4_fast_cb line=53 msg="enter fast path"

id=20085 trace_id=205 func=ip_session_run_all_tuple line=6750 msg="DNAT 10.7.7.20:8-
>192.168.11.100:8"
```

2.3.3 NAT configuration errors

In some cases, NAT operation cannot be performed correctly. One of such cases is configuration error. Let's analyze one example.

There is a host with IP 10.20.1.14. On the firewall there is a VIP configuration for this host with 'any' exit interface. The mapping in the VIP object for the incoming traffic is: "172.16.1.15-10.20.1.14". There is also another policy, which allows the host for the outgoing communication via different exit interface. The outgoing policy has a SNAT configured with a pool of IP addresses and one of them is 172.16.1.100.

The host on the left initiates the traffic and the source IP address is SNAT-ed to 172.16.1.100. The returning traffic should be DNAT-ed to the original host IP (10.20.1.14). Since we have a VIP with the same internal IP, the connection is reset by the firewall.

Figure 2.1

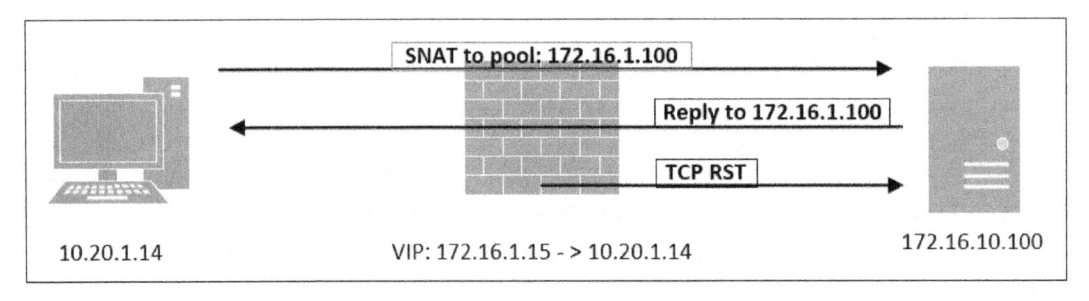

On the below output you can see the connection attempts without response (TCP SYN/ACK):

Example 2.36

```
forti # diagnose sniffer packet any  'host 10.20.1.14' 4
interfaces=[any]
filters=[host 10.20.1.14]
8.733836 VLAN 10 in 10.20.1.14.64874 -> 172.16.10.100.443: syn 1046817360
11.729096 VLAN 10 in 10.20.1.14.64874 -> 172.16.10.100.443: syn 1046817360
```

```
17.729078 VLAN 10 in 10.20.1.14.64874 -> 172.16.10.100.443: syn 1046817360
29.735967 VLAN 10 in 10.20.1.14.64875 -> 172.16.10.100.443: syn 166497838
32.736277 VLAN 10 in 10.20.1.14.64875 -> 172.16.10.100.443: syn 166497838
38.737069 VLAN 10 in 10.20.1.14.64875 -> 172.16.10.100.443: syn 166497838
```

When you analyze the "debug flow" output, you can notice the FortiGate sends RST packet:

Example 2.37

```
id=20085 trace_id=215 func=print_pkt_detail line=5375 msg="vd-root received a
packet(proto=6, 10.20.1.14:49651->172.16.10.100:443) from VLAN 10. flag [S], seq 1411922454,
ack 0, win 8192"

id=20085 trace_id=215 func=resolve_ip_tuple_fast line=5450 msg="Find an existing session,
id-051ac93e, original direction"

id=20085 trace_id=215 func=vf_ip_route_input_common line=2574 msg="find a route:
flag=00000000 gw-172.16.1.254 via VLAN 20"

id=20085 trace_id=215 func=__ip_session_run_tuple line=3282 msg="SNAT 10.20.1.14-
>172.16.1.100:49651"


id=20085 trace_id=216 func=print_pkt_detail line=5375 msg="vd-root received a
packet(proto=6, 172.16.10.100:443->172.16.1.100:49651) from VLAN 20. flag [S.], seq
2541017541, ack 1411922455, win 8192"

id=20085 trace_id=216 func=resolve_ip_tuple_fast line=5450 msg="Find an existing session,
id-051ac93e, reply direction"

id=20085 trace_id=216 func=__ip_session_run_tuple line=3296 msg="DNAT 172.16.1.100:49651-
>10.20.1.14:49651"

id=20085 trace_id=216 func=vf_ip_route_input_common line=2574 msg="find a route:
flag=80000000 gw-10.20.1.14 via root"


id=20085 trace_id=217 func=print_pkt_detail line=5375 msg="vd-root received a
packet(proto=6, 10.20.1.14:49651->172.16.10.100:443) from local. flag [R], seq 1411922455,
ack 0, win 0"

id=20085 trace_id=217 func=resolve_ip_tuple_fast line=5450 msg="Find an existing session,
id-051ac93e, original direction"

id=20085 trace_id=217 func=__ip_session_run_tuple line=3282 msg="SNAT 10.20.1.14-
>172.16.1.100:49651"
```

This can be corrected by avoiding VIP definition with 'any' interface. If you need to allow communication via different interfaces:

- incoming traffic: port1->port6
- outgoing traffic: port6->port2

try to be very specific when you create VIP objects.

Depending on the firmware version and NAT mode, outgoing traffic can be SNAT-ed to VIP. It means, SNAT settings in the firewall policy are overwritten by the VIP.

2.4 Central NAT

In Central NAT you separate firewall policies from the NAT. Once you enable it, separate tables for SNAT policies and DNAT definition are added. From the troubleshooting perspective there is no difference on how to proceed.

2.4.1 Source NAT

The connection generates the same information as with firewall policy NAT during the troubleshooting. There is just one more piece of configuration:

Example 2.38

```
forti # show firewall central-snat-map
config firewall central-snat-map
    edit 1
        set orig-addr "all"
        set srcintf "port5"
        set dst-addr "all"
        set dstintf "port2"
```

```
        set nat-ippool "test-nat-ip-pool"
    next
end
```

Both source IP addresses, before and after SNAT operation, are shown:

Example 2.39

```
forti # get system session list


PROTO    EXPIRE  SOURCE                   SOURCE-NAT           DESTINATION         DESTINATION-NAT

tcp      3596    192.168.11.100:49568     172.16.1.1:49568     172.217.14.206:80   -
```


I will not repeat **diagnose debug flow** as the output is the same, as shown in the examples 2.27-2.29

2.4.2 Destination NAT

There is one place in the **diagnose debug flow**, where you can spot the Central NAT is configured:

Example 2.40

```
id=20085 trace_id=175 func=print_pkt_detail line=5497 msg="vd-root:0 received a
packet(proto=6, 10.5.5.1:49321->172.16.1.250:80) from port2. flag [S], seq 4222690550, ack
0, win 8192"

id=20085 trace_id=175 func=init_ip_session_common line=5657 msg="allocate a new session-
000003e3"

id=20085 trace_id=175 func=fw_pre_route_handler line=182 msg="VIP-192.168.11.100:80, outdev-
unkown"

id=20085 trace_id=175 func=__ip_session_run_tuple line=3342 msg="DNAT 172.16.1.250:80-
>192.168.11.100:80"
```

```
id=20085 trace_id=175 func=vf_ip_route_input_common line=2591 msg="find a route:
flag=00000000 gw-192.168.11.100 via port5"

id=20085 trace_id=175 func=fw_snat_check line=466 msg="NAT disabled by central SNAT policy!"

id=20085 trace_id=175 func=fw_forward_handler line=751 msg="Allowed by Policy-2:"
```

Usually we do not need to perform SNAT for the incoming traffic. Once the destination IP is NAT-ed, FortiGate forwards the packet to the destination with its original source IP. If for some reasons you need to do SNAT, the output looks like the below example.

Example 2.41

```
id=20085 trace_id=75 func=print_pkt_detail line=5497 msg="vd-root:0 received a
packet(proto=6, 10.5.5.1:49288->172.16.1.250:80) from port2. flag [S], seq 452580924, ack 0,
win 8192"

id=20085 trace_id=75 func=init_ip_session_common line=5657 msg="allocate a new session-
0000037b"

id=20085 trace_id=75 func=fw_pre_route_handler line=182 msg="VIP-192.168.11.100:80, outdev-
unkown"

id=20085 trace_id=75 func=__ip_session_run_tuple line=3342 msg="DNAT 172.16.1.250:80-
>192.168.11.100:80"

id=20085 trace_id=75 func=vf_ip_route_input_common line=2591 msg="find a route:
flag=00000000 gw-192.168.11.100 via port5"

id=20085 trace_id=75 func=fw_forward_handler line=751 msg="Allowed by Policy-2: SNAT"

id=20085 trace_id=75 func=__ip_session_run_tuple line=3328 msg="SNAT 10.5.5.1-
>192.168.11.254:49288"
```

First packet (TCP SYN) and the order of operations:

- packet receives - 10.5.5.1:49288->172.16.1.250:80
- allocate new session
- VIP mapping found – VIP-192.168.11.100
- perform DNAT - 172.16.1.250:80->192.168.11.100:80
- find a route - gw-192.168.11.100 via port5
- check firewall policies – allowed by policy-2
- perform SNAT - 10.5.5.1->192.168.11.254:49288 – to hide a real source IP

In the reply packet (TCP SYN/ACK), there are following details:

- packet received
- find an existing session
- DNAT – what de facto is reverse of SNAT performed earlier
- find a route
- SNAT – reverse of DNAT applied earlier

Example 2.42

```
id=20085 trace_id=76 func=print_pkt_detail line=5497 msg="vd-root:0 received a packet(proto=6, 192.168.11.100:80->192.168.11.254:49288) from port5. flag [S.], seq 1595822326, ack 452580925, win 8192"

id=20085 trace_id=76 func=resolve_ip_tuple_fast line=5572 msg="Find an existing session, id-0000037b, reply direction"

id=20085 trace_id=76 func=__ip_session_run_tuple line=3342 msg="DNAT 192.168.11.254:49288->10.5.5.1:49288"

id=20085 trace_id=76 func=vf_ip_route_input_common line=2591 msg="find a route: flag=04000000 gw-172.16.1.254 via port2"

id=20085 trace_id=76 func=__ip_session_run_tuple line=3328 msg="SNAT 192.168.11.100->172.16.1.250:80"
```

In the last TCP ACK we can see:

- packet received
- find an existing session
- DNAT
- SNAT

Example 2.43

```
id=20085 trace_id=77 func=print_pkt_detail line=5497 msg="vd-root:0 received a packet(proto=6, 10.5.5.1:49288->172.16.1.250:80) from port2. flag [.], seq 452580925, ack 1595822327, win 4106"

id=20085 trace_id=77 func=resolve_ip_tuple_fast line=5572 msg="Find an existing session, id-0000037b, original direction"
```

```
id=20085 trace_id=77 func=__ip_session_run_tuple line=3342 msg="DNAT 172.16.1.250:80-
>192.168.11.100:80"

id=20085 trace_id=77 func=__ip_session_run_tuple line=3328 msg="SNAT 10.5.5.1-
>192.168.11.254:49288"
```

Try to avoid SNAT for the incoming traffic. It takes resources from the FortiGate firewall to manage this additional IP address translation.

2.5 Policy Lookup

In FortiOS 5.6 Policy Lookup was introduced. It gives you the ability to set parameters of the traffic and check if there is any matching firewall policy. It can help you, when traffic does not hit the policy as expected.

Figure 2.2

Policy Lookup	
Source Interface	
Protocol	IP
Protocol Number	1-255
Source	IP Address
Destination	IP Address/FQDN

Search   Cancel

3 Traffic Inspection

New Generation Firewalls (NGFW) protect your network much better than legacy models. They have the ability not only to inspect the traffic based on transport protocol and port number, but also based on the signatures. In next few sections I will present how to troubleshoot the most common problems.

3.1 Inspection mode

FortiGate can work in proxy or flow-based inspection mode. From FortiOS version 5.6, flow-based inspection is set by default. Before, proxy-based inspection was set. Up to FortiOS version 6.0, you set the inspection mode per a device or per VDOM, if enabled. There are a couple of security features on FortiGate, and some of them are available only in proxy-based inspection mode (check official documentation). FortiGate in flow-based inspection mode can do inspection only in the flow-based mode which is set in general settings. If your device is set to proxy-based inspection mode, depending on a specific security feature, it can perform inspection in proxy or flow mode. IPS engine which is used for IPS, Application Control, Antivirus (flow mode), performs inspection only in flow mode, even the FortiGate is set to proxy-based inspection.

Before we move on, I would like you to understand what the main difference between flow and proxy-based inspection is. Proxy-based inspection forwards the connection to the server, once TCP 3-way handshake is completed.

Figure 3.1

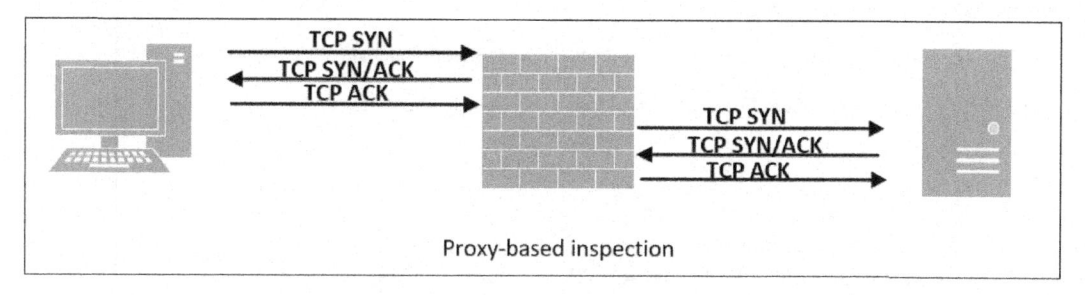

Proxy-based inspection

In the flow-based inspection mode, TCP session is established between the client and the server:

Figure 3.2

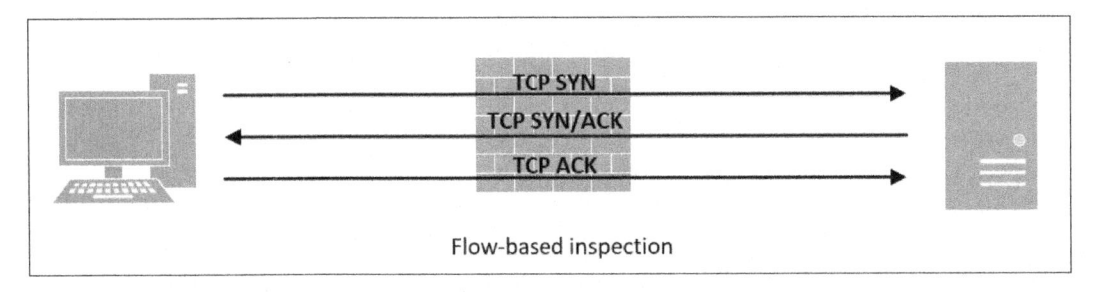

Flow-based inspection

In case of TCP SYN flood attack, the firewall in the proxy-based inspection mode protects the server resources. It does not forward incomplete TCP sessions.

In the below example you can see two TCP 3-way handshake exchange:

- first, between the client and FortiGate:

Example 3.1

```
id=20085 trace_id=10 func=print_pkt_detail line=5497 msg="vd-root:0 received a
packet(proto=6, 192.168.11.100:49531->13.56.33.144:80) from port5. flag [S], seq 4196437253,
ack 0, win 8192"

id=20085 trace_id=10 func=init_ip_session_common line=5657 msg="allocate a new session-
000004ff"

id=20085 trace_id=10 func=vf_ip_route_input_common line=2591 msg="find a route:
flag=04000000 gw-172.16.1.254 via port2"

id=20085 trace_id=10 func=fw_forward_handler line=751 msg="Allowed by Policy-1: AV SNAT"

id=20085 trace_id=10 func=av_receive line=301 msg="send to application layer"



id=20085 trace_id=11 func=print_pkt_detail line=5497 msg="vd-root:0 received a
packet(proto=6, 13.56.33.144:80->192.168.11.100:49531) from local. flag [S.], seq 165166478,
ack 4196437254, win 14600"
```

```
id=20085 trace_id=11 func=resolve_ip_tuple_fast line=5572 msg="Find an existing session, id-
000004ff, reply direction"


id=20085 trace_id=12 func=print_pkt_detail line=5497 msg="vd-root:0 received a
packet(proto=6, 192.168.11.100:49531->13.56.33.144:80) from port5. flag [.], seq 4196437254,
ack 165166479, win 2053"

id=20085 trace_id=12 func=resolve_ip_tuple_fast line=5572 msg="Find an existing session, id-
000004ff, original direction"

id=20085 trace_id=12 func=av_receive line=301 msg="send to application layer"
```

- second, between FortiGate and the server:

Example 3.2

```
id=20085 trace_id=13 func=print_pkt_detail line=5497 msg="vd-root:0 received a
packet(proto=6, 192.168.11.100:49531->13.56.33.144:80) from local. flag [S], seq 1792376582,
ack 0, win 14600"

id=20085 trace_id=13 func=resolve_ip_tuple_fast line=5572 msg="Find an existing session, id-
000004ff, original direction"

id=20085 trace_id=13 func=__ip_session_run_tuple line=3328 msg="SNAT 192.168.11.100-
>172.16.1.1:49531"


id=20085 trace_id=16 func=print_pkt_detail line=5497 msg="vd-root:0 received a
packet(proto=6, 13.56.33.144:80->172.16.1.1:49531) from port2. flag [S.], seq 2195708818,
ack 1792376583, win 16060"

id=20085 trace_id=16 func=resolve_ip_tuple_fast line=5572 msg="Find an existing session, id-
000004ff, reply direction"

id=20085 trace_id=16 func=__ip_session_run_tuple line=3342 msg="DNAT 172.16.1.1:49531-
>192.168.11.100:49531"

id=20085 trace_id=16 func=vf_ip_route_input_common line=2591 msg="find a route:
flag=00000000 gw-192.168.11.100 via port5"

id=20085 trace_id=16 func=av_receive line=301 msg="send to application layer"
```

```
id=20085 trace_id=17 func=print_pkt_detail line=5497 msg="vd-root:0 received a
packet(proto=6, 192.168.11.100:49531->13.56.33.144:80) from local. flag [.], seq 1792376583,
ack 2195708819, win 3650"

id=20085 trace_id=17 func=resolve_ip_tuple_fast line=5572 msg="Find an existing session, id-
000004ff, original direction"

id=20085 trace_id=17 func=__ip_session_run_tuple line=3328 msg="SNAT 192.168.11.100-
>172.16.1.1:49531"
```

Once the session is established, it can be visible in the output of **diagnose sys session list**:

- proxy-based inspection mode – one of the sessions is in 'redir' state:

Example 3.3

```
session info: proto=6 proto_state=11 duration=8 expire=3592 timeout=3600 flags=00000000
sockflag=00000000 sockport=443 av_idx=9 use=6

origin-shaper=

reply-shaper=

per_ip_shaper=

class_id=0 ha_id=0 policy_dir=0 tunnel=/ vlan_cos=0/255

state=redir log local may_dirty nlb f00

statistic(bytes/packets/allow_err): org=164/3/1 reply=92/2/1 tuples=3

tx speed(Bps/kbps): 20/0 rx speed(Bps/kbps): 11/0

orgin->sink: org pre->post, reply pre->post dev=5->3/3->5 gwy=172.16.1.254/192.168.11.100

hook=post dir=org act=snat 192.168.11.100:49760->151.101.1.164:443(172.16.1.1:49760)

hook=pre dir=reply act=dnat 151.101.1.164:443->172.16.1.1:49760(192.168.11.100:49760)

hook=post dir=reply act=noop 151.101.1.164:443->192.168.11.100:49760(0.0.0.0:0)

pos/(before,after) 0/(0,0), 0/(0,0)

misc=0 policy_id=1 auth_info=0 chk_client_info=0 vd=0

serial=00000711 tos=40/40 app_list=0 app=0 url_cat=0

rpdb_link_id = 00000000
```

- flow-based inspection mode – in the state of the session you should see 'ndr':

Example 3.4

```
session info: proto=6 proto_state=66 duration=3 expire=2 timeout=3600 flags=00000000
sockflag=00000000 sockport=443 av_idx=0 use=5
origin-shaper=
reply-shaper=
per_ip_shaper=
class_id=0 ha_id=0 policy_dir=0 tunnel=/ vlan_cos=0/255
state=log may_dirty ndr nlb f00
statistic(bytes/packets/allow_err): org=1213/14/1 reply=8357/16/0 tuples=3
tx speed(Bps/kbps): 400/3 rx speed(Bps/kbps): 2758/22
orgin->sink: org pre->post, reply pre->post dev=5->3/3->5 gwy=172.16.1.254/192.168.11.100
hook=post dir=org act=snat 192.168.11.100:49979->151.101.1.164:443(172.16.1.1:49979)
hook=pre dir=reply act=dnat 151.101.1.164:443->172.16.1.1:49979(192.168.11.100:49979)
hook=post dir=reply act=noop 151.101.1.164:443->192.168.11.100:49979(0.0.0.0:0)
pos/(before,after) 0/(0,0), 0/(0,0)
misc=0 policy_id=1 auth_info=0 chk_client_info=0 vd=0
serial=00000838 tos=ff/ff app_list=0 app=0 url_cat=0
rpdb_link_id = 00000000
dd_type=0 dd_mode=0
```

3.2 Web Filtering

Web filtering controls what types of web categories should be permitted. You can build general or dedicated policies for specific group of users. The main verification tool is of course the log message. Always start by checking what is there. If something does not work as expected, you can check the connection by verifying the output from the following commands:

Example 3.5

```
diagnose debug urlfilter src-addr <IP>
diagnose debug urlfilter test-url <url>
diagnose debug application urlfilter -1
diagnose debug enable
```

In the below example there is a request for 'www.fortinet.com'. Traffic is not encrypted (http) and the action is 'monitor'. In the last line you can see web category: 52, which represents 'IT':

Example 3.6

```
msg="received a request /tmp/.ipsengine_536_0_0.url.socket, addr_len=37:
d=www.fortinet.com:80, id=508, cat=255, vfname='root', vfid=0, profile='default', type=0,
client=192.168.11.100, url_source=1, url="/"

msg="Cache miss" user="N/A" src=192.168.11.100 sport=50841 dst=13.56.33.144 dport=80
service="http" hostname="www.fortinet.com" url="/"

action=12(ftgd-monitor) wf-act=0(MONITOR) user="N/A" src=192.168.11.100 sport=50841
dst=13.56.33.144 dport=80 service="http" cat=52 hostname="www.fortinet.com" url="/"
```

The next example is 'https' traffic, and that is why 'url_source=3', which is the Server Name Indication (SNI). This is an extension of the TLS protocol. The hostname is 'bing.com' and the action is 'block'. Web category is '41' – 'Search Engines and Portals':

Example 3.7

```
msg="received a request /tmp/.ipsengine_536_0_0.url.socket, addr_len=37: d=c.bing.com:443,
id=516, cat=255, vfname='root', vfid=0, profile='default', type=1, client=192.168.11.100,
url_source=3, url="/"

msg="Cache miss" user="N/A" src=192.168.11.100 sport=50893 dst=13.107.21.200 dport=443
service="https" hostname="c.bing.com" url="/"
```

```
action=10(ftgd-block) wf-act=3(BLOCK) user="N/A" src=192.168.11.100 sport=50893
dst=13.107.21.200 dport=443 service="https" cat=41 hostname="c.bing.com" url="/"
```

In the last example 'http' traffic: url_source=1 means 'HTTP header'. The hostname is 'www.nytimes.com' and web category is '36' – 'News and Media':

Example 3.8

```
msg="received a request /tmp/.ipsengine_536_0_0.url.socket, addr_len=37:
d=www.nytimes.com:80, id=548, cat=255, vfname='root', vfid=0, profile='default', type=0,
client=192.168.11.100, url_source=1, url="/favicon.ico"

msg="Cache miss" user="N/A" src=192.168.11.100 sport=50955 dst=151.101.53.164 dport=80
service="http" hostname="www.nytimes.com" url="/favicon.ico"

action=10(ftgd-block) wf-act=3(BLOCK) user="N/A" src=192.168.11.100 sport=50955
dst=151.101.53.164 dport=80 service="http" cat=36 hostname="www.nytimes.com"
url="/favicon.ico"
```

The full list of categories can be found on docs.fortinet.com.

These are the four possible values of 'url_source':

- '0' (A) – Unknown
- '1' (B) – HTTP Header
- '2' (C) – SNI Name
- '3' (D) – Server Certificate CN Name

There is one more diagnose tool available which allows to display or clear different cache types:

Example 3.9

```
Forti # diagnose debug application urlfilter 1


1.    This menu

2.    Clear WF cache
```

3.   Display WF cache contents
4.   Display WF cache TTL list
5.   Display WF cache RCU info
6.   Display WF cache in tree format
7.   Toggle switch for dumping unrated packet
10. Print debug values
11. Clear Spam Filter cache
12. Clear AV Query cache
13. Toggle switch for dumping expired license packets
14. Show running timers (except request timers)
144. Show running timers (including request timers)
15. Send INIT requests.
16. Display WF cache contents of prefix type
19. Display object counts
20. Display FTGD TCP stats
21. Display FTGD quota list
22. Reset all user quotas
99. Restart the urlfilter daemon.

Debug levels:
Warning messages:	1	(0x001)
Block events:	2	(0x002)
Pass events:	4	(0x004)
URL request events:	8	(0x008)
Cache events:	16	(0x010)
Prefix events:	32	(0x020)
Prefix delete subtree events:	64	(0x040)
Add after prefix events:	128	(0x080)
CMDB events:	256	(0x100)

```
DNS resolver messages:        512 (0x200)
Keyword search messages:     1024 (0x400)


forti # INIT request messages:    2048 (0x800)
Quota messages:              4096 (0x1000)
Per-user b/w list messages:  8192 (0x2000)



forti #
```

3.3 Antivirus

While working with FortiGate you may encounter problems with antivirus inspection. FortiGate can work in flow or proxy inspection mode. Depending on the settings there are different steps in the way the traffic is processed.

3.3.1 Flow-based inspection mode

There are some cons and pros between inspection modes. For Antivirus, the flow-based inspection is a primary choice due to the hardware acceleration. On the below outputs you can see a connection to eicar.org website, where you can test your antivirus system:

http://2016.eicar.org/download/eicar.com.txt

The file eicar.com.txt contains a malware test file, which should trigger the alarm. Note how the traffic is sent to the IPS engine for the inspection:

Example 3.10

```
id=20085 trace_id=12 func=print_pkt_detail line=5497 msg="vd-root:0 received a
packet(proto=6, 172.16.1.100:50834->213.211.198.58:80) from port3. flag [S], seq 2009704943,
ack 0, win 8192"
```

```
id=20085 trace_id=12 func=init_ip_session_common line=5657 msg="allocate a new session-00000d59"

id=20085 trace_id=12 func=vf_ip_route_input_common line=2591 msg="find a route: flag=04000000 gw-172.16.10.254 via port1"

id=20085 trace_id=12 func=fw_forward_handler line=751 msg="Allowed by Policy-172: SNAT"

id=20085 trace_id=12 func=ids_receive line=285 msg="send to ips" <- flow-based inspection mode

id=20085 trace_id=12 func=__ip_session_run_tuple line=3328 msg="SNAT 172.16.1.100->172.16.10.1:50834"
```

Below are the diagnose commands required to see the inspection:

Example 3.11

```
diagnose debug application scanunit -1
diagnose debug enable
```

You can see the details of the inspection in the below output:

- client N/A server N/A – in flow-based inspection you do not see IP addresses
- object_name 'eicar.com.txt' – the file name to be scanned
- extended – type of the database (there are three options: normal, extended and extreme)
- scan file 'eicar.com.txt' – scan operation
- scan result – '1' means virus was found, '0' – no virus
- insert infection VIRUS SUCCEEDED...infection 1 – confirmation one infection was identified

Example 3.12

```
su 620 job 97 open
su 620 req vfid 0 id 120 ep 0 new request, size 68
su 620 req vfid 0 id 120 ep 0 received; ack 97, data type: 2
su 620 job 97 request info:
```

```
su 620 job 97    client N/A server N/A
su 620 job 97    object_name 'eicar.com.txt'
su 620 enable databases 07 (core mmdb extended)
su 620 scan file 'eicar.com.txt' bytes 68
su 620 scan result 1
su 620 not wanted for analytics: analytics submission is disabled (m 0 r 1)
su 620 add VIRUS infection
su 620 insert infection VIRUS SUCCEEDED loc (nil) off 0 sz 0 at index 0 total infections 1 error 0
su 620 job 97 send result
su 620 job 97 close
```

3.3.2 Proxy-based inspection mode

The proxy-based inspection is slower, as it cannot offload inspection to the ASICs. Remember that the scan effectiveness is the same, as the full file is checked in both inspection modes (except 'Quick' scan).

Note how the file is sent to the 'application layer' in the proxy-based inspection:

Example 3.13

```
id=20085 trace_id=21 func=print_pkt_detail line=5497 msg="vd-root:0 received a packet(proto=6, 172.16.1.100:50894->213.211.198.58:80) from port3. flag [S], seq 3492115526, ack 0, win 8192"

id=20085 trace_id=21 func=init_ip_session_common line=5657 msg="allocate a new session-00000def"

id=20085 trace_id=21 func=vf_ip_route_input_common line=2591 msg="find a route: flag=04000000 gw-172.16.10.254 via port1"

id=20085 trace_id=21 func=fw_forward_handler line=751 msg="Allowed by Policy-172: AV SNAT"

id=20085 trace_id=21 func=av_receive line=301 msg="send to application layer"<-proxy-based inspection mode
```

Check in the below output, there are more details presented in the 'proxy' mode:

- client/server – in proxy-based inspection you can see the client and the server IPs
- object_name – name of the object to be scanned
- extended – database type
- scan file 'eicar.com.txt' – scan process
- scan result 1 – virus was found
- infection VIRUS SUCCEEDED… infection 1 – confirmation one infection was found

Example 3.14

```
su 620 job 114 open

su 620 req vfid 0 id 16 ep 0 new request, size 355

su 620 req vfid 0 id 16 ep 0 received; ack 114, data type: 0

su 620 job 114 request info:

su 620 job 114    client 172.16.1.100:50954 server 213.211.198.58:80

su 620 job 114    object_name 'eicar.com.txt'

su 620 enable databases 07 (core mmdb extended)

su 620 job 114 begin http scan

su 620 scan file 'eicar.com.txt' bytes 68

su 620 scan result 1

su 620 job 114 end http scan

su 620 job 114 virus 'EICAR_TEST_FILE' cat 0 file 'eicar.com.txt' sig 359205 vnameid 2172 checksum 6851cf3c size 68 sha 275a021bbfb6489e54d471899f7db9d1663fc695ec2fe2a2c4538aabf651fd0f av mon 0 quar 'n/a' quar_skip 3

su 620 add VIRUS infection

su 620 insert infection VIRUS SUCCEEDED loc (nil) off 0 sz 0 at index 0 total infections 1 error 0

su 620 not wanted for analytics: analytics submission is disabled (m 0 r 1)

su 620 job 114 send result

su 620 job 114 close
```

3.4 IPS

All inspections which use IPS engine are performed in the flow-based inspection mode. Below there is an example of an attack mitigated by IPS. In the **diagnose debug flow** output there is a message: "send to ips":

Example 3.15

```
id=20085 trace_id=1 func=print_pkt_detail line=5497 msg="vd-root:0 received a packet(proto=6, 172.16.10.254:57150->172.16.10.200:80) from port5. flag [S], seq 1783637709, ack 0, win 29200"

id=20085 trace_id=1 func=init_ip_session_common line=5657 msg="allocate a new session-00000744"

id=20085 trace_id=1 func=fw_pre_route_handler line=182 msg="VIP-10.2.20.100:80, outdev-port5"

id=20085 trace_id=1 func=__ip_session_run_tuple line=3342 msg="DNAT 172.16.10.200:80->10.2.20.100:80"

id=20085 trace_id=1 func=vf_ip_route_input_common line=2591 msg="find a route: flag=04000000 gw-10.2.20.100 via port2"

id=20085 trace_id=1 func=fw_forward_handler line=751 msg="Allowed by Policy-28:"

id=20085 trace_id=1 func=ids_receive line=285 msg="send to ips" <- IPS security profile is enabled
```

It is important to check the IPS engine and its logs. The below commands show you how the threats are identified:

Example 3.16

```
diagnose debug application ipsengine -1
diagnose debug enable
```

In the following output you can see:

- Policy ID
- client - direction of the attack
- attack_id
- fds – FortiGuard Distribution Server attack ID
- log IPS ID

Example 3.17

```
packet: vf:0 vrf:0 policy:28 view:0 size:204 from: client
(xlr--1) log request 1
attack_id=71036 app=0 client=1 opaque=0x2 dir=2
fds 71036
log ips 71036
```

There is one more tool which can help you with the IPS engine. You can choose one of the options to select the desired action. When you type the question mark '?' it shows the list with all parameters:

Example 3.18

```
forti # diagnose test application ipsmonitor ?


IPS Engine Test Usage:


    1: Display IPS engine information
    2: Toggle IPS engine enable/disable status
    3: Display restart log
    4: Clear restart log
    5: Toggle bypass status
    6: Submit attack characteristics now
   10: IPS queue length
   11: Clear IPS queue length
```

```
12: IPS L7 socket statistics

13: IPS session list

14: IPS NTurbo statistics

15: IPSA statistics

18: Display session info cache

19: Clear session info cache

21: Reload FSA malicious URL database

22: Reload whitelist URL database

24: Display Flow AV statistics

25: Reset Flow AV statistics

96: Toggle IPS engines watchdog timer

97: Start all IPS engines

98: Stop all IPS engines

99: Restart all IPS engines and monitor

forti #
```

4 VPN

FortiGate supports both VPN types: IPsec and SSL VPN. There are many differences between them, from the implementation perspective and use case scenarios. IPsec is RFC standard (or framework of standards) and you should be able to establish a site-to-site VPN tunnel between different devices (different vendors).

4.1 IPsec

There are many reasons why VPN may not work. Below I present one example with no issues, then more examples with some errors. I analyze the **diagnose debug** output and show the most common problems and their symptoms.

4.1.1 Example #1

In the first example you can see the output of **diagnose debug** command, and what you should see when the tunnel is up. In this case the configuration is correct.

Example 4.1

```
diagnose debug application ike 255
diagnose debug enable
```

At the beginning you see the initial packets sent:

Example 4.2

```
ike 0:VPNtoSite2:1: sent IKE msg (quick_i1send): 172.16.2.1:500->172.16.3.1:500, len=620,
id=78d8df4db8a62810/f36dccd009c4a966:ab5acdef
ike 0: comes 172.16.3.1:500->172.16.2.1:500,ifindex=4....
```

```
ike 0: IKEv1 exchange=Quick id=78d8df4db8a62810/f36dccd009c4a966:ab5acdef len=444
ike 0: in
...
ike 0:VPNtoSite2:1:VPNtoSite2:0: responder selectors 0:10.0.1.0/255.255.255.0:0-
>0:10.0.2.0/255.255.255.0:0
```

and then there are "my proposals", which are the parameters to agree in order to establish IKE phase1:

Example 4.3

```
ike 0:VPNtoSite2:1:VPNtoSite2:0: my proposal:
ike 0:VPNtoSite2:1:VPNtoSite2:0: proposal id = 1:
ike 0:VPNtoSite2:1:VPNtoSite2:0:    protocol id = IPSEC_ESP:
ike 0:VPNtoSite2:1:VPNtoSite2:0:    PFS DH group = 14
ike 0:VPNtoSite2:1:VPNtoSite2:0:       trans_id = ESP_AES_CBC (key_len = 128)
ike 0:VPNtoSite2:1:VPNtoSite2:0:       encapsulation = ENCAPSULATION_MODE_TUNNEL
ike 0:VPNtoSite2:1:VPNtoSite2:0:          type = AUTH_ALG, val=SHA1
ike 0:VPNtoSite2:1:VPNtoSite2:0:       trans_id = ESP_AES_CBC (key_len = 256)
ike 0:VPNtoSite2:1:VPNtoSite2:0:       encapsulation = ENCAPSULATION_MODE_TUNNEL
ike 0:VPNtoSite2:1:VPNtoSite2:0:          type = AUTH_ALG, val=SHA1
ike 0:VPNtoSite2:1:VPNtoSite2:0:       trans_id = ESP_AES_CBC (key_len = 128)
ike 0:VPNtoSite2:1:VPNtoSite2:0:       encapsulation = ENCAPSULATION_MODE_TUNNEL
ike 0:VPNtoSite2:1:VPNtoSite2:0:          type = AUTH_ALG, val=SHA2_256
ike 0:VPNtoSite2:1:VPNtoSite2:0:       trans_id = ESP_AES_CBC (key_len = 256)
ike 0:VPNtoSite2:1:VPNtoSite2:0:       encapsulation = ENCAPSULATION_MODE_TUNNEL
ike 0:VPNtoSite2:1:VPNtoSite2:0:          type = AUTH_ALG, val=SHA2_256
ike 0:VPNtoSite2:1:VPNtoSite2:0:       trans_id = ESP_AES_GCM_16 (key_len = 128)
ike 0:VPNtoSite2:1:VPNtoSite2:0:       encapsulation = ENCAPSULATION_MODE_TUNNEL
ike 0:VPNtoSite2:1:VPNtoSite2:0:          type = AUTH_ALG, val=NULL
```

```
ike 0:VPNtoSite2:1:VPNtoSite2:0:         trans_id = ESP_AES_GCM_16 (key_len = 256)
ike 0:VPNtoSite2:1:VPNtoSite2:0:         encapsulation = ENCAPSULATION_MODE_TUNNEL
ike 0:VPNtoSite2:1:VPNtoSite2:0:            type = AUTH_ALG, val=NULL
ike 0:VPNtoSite2:1:VPNtoSite2:0:         trans_id = ESP_CHACHA20_POLY1305 (key_len = 256)
ike 0:VPNtoSite2:1:VPNtoSite2:0:         encapsulation = ENCAPSULATION_MODE_TUNNEL
ike 0:VPNtoSite2:1:VPNtoSite2:0:            type = AUTH_ALG, val=NULL
```

Next, the incoming proposals from the VPN gateway:

Example 4.4

```
ike 0:VPNtoSite2:1:VPNtoSite2:0: incoming proposal:
ike 0:VPNtoSite2:1:VPNtoSite2:0: proposal id = 1:
ike 0:VPNtoSite2:1:VPNtoSite2:0:   protocol id = IPSEC_ESP:
ike 0:VPNtoSite2:1:VPNtoSite2:0:   PFS DH group = 14
ike 0:VPNtoSite2:1:VPNtoSite2:0:      trans_id = ESP_AES_CBC (key_len = 128)
ike 0:VPNtoSite2:1:VPNtoSite2:0:      encapsulation = ENCAPSULATION_MODE_TUNNEL
ike 0:VPNtoSite2:1:VPNtoSite2:0:         type = AUTH_ALG, val=SHA1
```

and rest of the IPsec messages which are exchanged between VPN gateways:

Example 4.5

```
ike 0:VPNtoSite2: schedule auto-negotiate
ike 0:VPNtoSite2:1:VPNtoSite2:0: replay protection enabled
ike 0:VPNtoSite2:1:VPNtoSite2:0: SA life soft seconds=42900.
ike 0:VPNtoSite2:1:VPNtoSite2:0: SA life hard seconds=43200.
ike 0:VPNtoSite2:1:VPNtoSite2:0: IPsec SA selectors #src=1 #dst=1
ike 0:VPNtoSite2:1:VPNtoSite2:0: src 0 4 0:10.0.1.0/255.255.255.0:0 <- selectors are part of phase2
```

```
ike 0:VPNtoSite2:1:VPNtoSite2:0: dst 0 4 0:10.0.2.0/255.255.255.0:0 <- selectors are part of
phase2

ike 0:VPNtoSite2:1:VPNtoSite2:0: add IPsec SA: SPIs=a846d30c/9b32fda3

ike 0:VPNtoSite2:1:VPNtoSite2:0: IPsec SA dec spi a846d30c key
16:3BB66576EF4EE16F50E84E496FFE3331 auth 20:E109F5462BEFB3886C4F16B0B4F485125B448C98

ike 0:VPNtoSite2:1:VPNtoSite2:0: IPsec SA enc spi 9b32fda3 key
16:BFB680134CD52DBFC80517D3B7D089E7 auth 20:81CAB5A55C9F45E326CE503E1A4056CF2868502F
```

Finally, the confirmation that the tunnel is up:

Example 4.6

```
ike 0:VPNtoSite2:1:VPNtoSite2:0: added IPsec SA: SPIs=a846d30c/9b32fda3

ike 0:VPNtoSite2:1:VPNtoSite2:0: sending SNMP tunnel UP trap

ike 0:VPNtoSite2:1: enc
78D8DF4DB8A62810F36DCCD009C4A96608102001AB5ACDEF0000004000000024EB1236D547DCD5151A133E5D4D20
FC7EB0E3028704537083F63FC80DB98D56AD

ike 0:VPNtoSite2:1: out
78D8DF4DB8A62810F36DCCD009C4A96608102001AB5ACDEF0000004CEB35C332B0CE97FFD33B47DC27E62E3279D9
E232087CF1E1FA40C69EE6D14FA5843B858500618CF543266FF735ABE595
```

This is what we see on the remote VPN gateway:

Example 4.7

```
ike 0: comes 172.16.2.1:500->172.16.3.1:500,ifindex=6....

ike 0: IKEv1 exchange=Quick id=78d8df4db8a62810/f36dccd009c4a966:ab5acdef len=620

...

ike 0:VPNtoSite1:0:0: responder received first quick-mode message

...

ike 0:VPNtoSite1:0:0: peer proposal is: peer:0:10.0.1.0-10.0.1.255:0, me:0:10.0.2.0-
10.0.2.255:0

ike 0:VPNtoSite1:0:VPNtoSite1:0: trying

ike 0:VPNtoSite1:0:VPNtoSite1:0: matched phase2
```

```
ike 0:VPNtoSite1:0:VPNtoSite1:0: autokey
```

There are couple of proposals sent, with many algorithms. I have removed some of them for readability:

Example 4.8

```
ike 0:VPNtoSite1:0:VPNtoSite1:0: my proposal:
ike 0:VPNtoSite1:0:VPNtoSite1:0: proposal id = 1:
ike 0:VPNtoSite1:0:VPNtoSite1:0:    protocol id = IPSEC_ESP:
ike 0:VPNtoSite1:0:VPNtoSite1:0:    PFS DH group = 14
ike 0:VPNtoSite1:0:VPNtoSite1:0:      trans_id = ESP_AES_CBC (key_len = 128)
ike 0:VPNtoSite1:0:VPNtoSite1:0:      encapsulation = ENCAPSULATION_MODE_TUNNEL
ike 0:VPNtoSite1:0:VPNtoSite1:0:        type = AUTH_ALG, val=SHA1
ike 0:VPNtoSite1:0:VPNtoSite1:0:      trans_id = ESP_AES_CBC (key_len = 256)
ike 0:VPNtoSite1:0:VPNtoSite1:0:      encapsulation = ENCAPSULATION_MODE_TUNNEL
ike 0:VPNtoSite1:0:VPNtoSite1:0:        type = AUTH_ALG, val=SHA1
...
ike 0:VPNtoSite1:0:VPNtoSite1:0: proposal id = 2:
ike 0:VPNtoSite1:0:VPNtoSite1:0:    protocol id = IPSEC_ESP:
ike 0:VPNtoSite1:0:VPNtoSite1:0:    PFS DH group = 5
ike 0:VPNtoSite1:0:VPNtoSite1:0:      trans_id = ESP_AES_CBC (key_len = 128)
ike 0:VPNtoSite1:0:VPNtoSite1:0:      encapsulation = ENCAPSULATION_MODE_TUNNEL
ike 0:VPNtoSite1:0:VPNtoSite1:0:        type = AUTH_ALG, val=SHA1
...
ike 0:VPNtoSite1:0:VPNtoSite1:0: incoming proposal:
ike 0:VPNtoSite1:0:VPNtoSite1:0: proposal id = 1:
ike 0:VPNtoSite1:0:VPNtoSite1:0:    protocol id = IPSEC_ESP:
ike 0:VPNtoSite1:0:VPNtoSite1:0:    PFS DH group = 14
ike 0:VPNtoSite1:0:VPNtoSite1:0:      trans_id = ESP_AES_CBC (key_len = 128)
```

```
ike 0:VPNtoSite1:0:VPNtoSite1:0:         encapsulation = ENCAPSULATION_MODE_TUNNEL
ike 0:VPNtoSite1:0:VPNtoSite1:0:           type = AUTH_ALG, val=SHA1
```

Next, the negotiation results and the final confirmation that the tunnel is up:

Example 4.9

```
ike 0:VPNtoSite1:0:VPNtoSite1:0: negotiation result
ike 0:VPNtoSite1:0:VPNtoSite1:0: proposal id = 1:
ike 0:VPNtoSite1:0:VPNtoSite1:0:     protocol id = IPSEC_ESP:
ike 0:VPNtoSite1:0:VPNtoSite1:0:     PFS DH group = 14
ike 0:VPNtoSite1:0:VPNtoSite1:0:        trans_id = ESP_AES_CBC (key_len = 128)
ike 0:VPNtoSite1:0:VPNtoSite1:0:        encapsulation = ENCAPSULATION_MODE_TUNNEL
ike 0:VPNtoSite1:0:VPNtoSite1:0:          type = AUTH_ALG, val=SHA1
ike 0:VPNtoSite1:0:VPNtoSite1:0: set pfs=MODP2048
ike 0:VPNtoSite1:0:VPNtoSite1:0: using tunnel mode.
ike 0:VPNtoSite1: schedule auto-negotiate
ike 0:VPNtoSite1:0:VPNtoSite1:0: replay protection enabled
ike 0:VPNtoSite1:0:VPNtoSite1:0: SA life soft seconds=42927.
ike 0:VPNtoSite1:0:VPNtoSite1:0: SA life hard seconds=43200.
ike 0:VPNtoSite1:0:VPNtoSite1:0: IPsec SA selectors #src=1 #dst=1
ike 0:VPNtoSite1:0:VPNtoSite1:0: src 0 7 0:10.0.2.0-10.0.2.255:0
ike 0:VPNtoSite1:0:VPNtoSite1:0: dst 0 7 0:10.0.1.0-10.0.1.255:0
ike 0:VPNtoSite1:0:VPNtoSite1:0: add IPsec SA: SPIs=9b32fda3/a846d30c
ike 0:VPNtoSite1:0:VPNtoSite1:0: IPsec SA dec spi 9b32fda3 key
16:BFB680134CD52DBFC80517D3B7D089E7 auth 20:81CAB5A55C9F45E326CE503E1A4056CF2868502F
ike 0:VPNtoSite1:0:VPNtoSite1:0: IPsec SA enc spi a846d30c key
16:3BB66576EF4EE16F50E84E496FFE3331 auth 20:E109F5462BEFB3886C4F16B0B4F485125B448C98
ike 0:VPNtoSite1:0:VPNtoSite1:0: added IPsec SA: SPIs=9b32fda3/a846d30c
ike 0:VPNtoSite1:0:VPNtoSite1:0: sending SNMP tunnel UP trap
```

You may need also to check or investigate the tunnels that are up and working fine. Below there are some useful commands with their outputs. Some of them present the same or similar information, but with different level of details.

Example 4.10

```
FG-A # diagnose vpn ike gateway list


vd: root/0   <- VDOM name
name: VPNtoSite2
version: 1
interface: port2 4
addr: 172.16.2.1:500 -> 172.16.3.1:500   <- Peer IPs
created: 91s ago
IKE SA: created 2/2   established 2/2   time 0/10520/21040 ms
IPsec SA: created 1/1   established 1/1   time 0/0/0 ms

  id/spi: 7 f1d8ca6090b7d820/8363512edae52f5d
  direction: responder <- role (initiator/responder)
  status: established 72-72s ago = 0ms
  proposal: aes256-sha1 <- selected proposal
  key: 4be504c31e1d0928-8102a051492a07c6-b675e85229ef2bb0-4c9f618bd9e7053f
  lifetime/rekey: 86400/86057
  DPD sent/recv: 00000000/00000000

  id/spi: 4 65482aeeb7cb95ce/dcdb0f7817f1edd6
  direction: initiator
  status: established 91-70s ago = 21040ms
  proposal: aes256-sha1
```

```
  key: 865179f9b28494aa-1929b66e41e337bb-fdfa4dbc0de298ca-21dbe27b2cfbc310

  lifetime/rekey: 86400/86030

  DPD sent/recv: 00000000/00000000


FG-A #
```

Example 4.11

```
FG-A # diagnose vpn tunnel list

list all ipsec tunnel in vd 0

------------------------------------------------------

name=VPNtoSite2 ver=1 serial=1 172.16.2.1:0->172.16.3.1:0 <- peer IPs

bound_if=4 lgwy=static/1 tun=intf/0 mode=auto/1 encap=none/0

proxyid_num=1 child_num=0 refcnt=12 ilast=18 olast=78 ad=/0

stat: rxp=8 txp=8 rxb=960 txb=480

dpd: mode=on-demand on=1 idle=20000ms retry=3 count=0 seqno=0 <- Dead Peer Detection

natt: mode=none draft=0 interval=0 remote_port=0

proxyid=VPNtoSite2 proto=0 sa=1 ref=2 serial=1

  src: 0:10.0.1.0/255.255.255.0:0 <- selectors

  dst: 0:10.0.2.0/255.255.255.0:0 <- selectors

  SA:  ref=3 options=10226 type=00 soft=0 mtu=1438 expire=42811/0B replaywin=2048

       seqno=9 esn=0 replaywin_lastseq=00000009 itn=0

  life: type=01 bytes=0/0 timeout=42902/43200

  dec: spi=ece57217 esp=aes key=16 7747288ff924a97c8754b3ff2c72837f

       ah=sha1 key=20 9be4eac54d718c03e24f013158a3087f5b564d5d

  enc: spi=9468e952 esp=aes key=16 44dccd823b56730473ed296fdf4f6433

       ah=sha1 key=20 f5d87b7372d179a357d28469e38fb915a147f1d0

  dec:pkts/bytes=8/480, enc:pkts/bytes=8/960


FG-A #
```

On devices with ASICs you can check if IPsec is offloaded. With hardware acceleration the encryption and decryption operations are performed faster. There will be one of the four flags:

- NPU_FLAG 00 – no hardware acceleration
- NPU_FLAG 01 – only egress packets
- NPU_FLAG 02 – only ingress packets
- NPU_FLAG 03 – both directions - as in the example below

Example 4.12

```
FG-A # diagnose vpn tunnel list
…
proxyid=partner02 proto=0 sa=1 ref=4 serial=10
  src: 0:192.168.10.0/255.255.255.0:0
  dst: 0:192.168.20.0/255.255.255.0:0
  SA:  ref=6 options=10026 type=00 soft=0 mtu=1446 expire=3249/0B replaywin=2048
       seqno=5 esn=0 replaywin_lastseq=00000001 itn=0
  life: type=01 bytes=0/0 timeout=3302/3600
  dec: spi=125b049f esp=3des key=24 d0931f2445a22f0d7bb750bccbe6aaa0264f2cea8690ab4c
       ah=md5 key=16 1734ee046f3261edd9d63086616b34e6
  enc: spi=c98985c6 esp=3des key=24 b3b6c06347aa3576ca41382ca6f16c3e6ed1fa9ab7e2ab9a
       ah=md5 key=16 9df84f05105fe16136ff0858f2ae7977
  dec:pkts/bytes=1/31, enc:pkts/bytes=4/992
  npu_flag=03 npu_rgwy=10.20.3.1 npu_lgwy=10.20.1.1 npu_selid=122 dec_npuid=2 enc_npuid=2
```

The command **get vpn ipsec tunnel details** is the most informative one. It shows a tunnel name, type (route or policy based), IKE version, local and remote gateway IPs, selectors, number of packets:

Example 4.13

```
FG-A # get vpn ipsec tunnel details


gateway
  name: 'VPNtoSite2'
  type: route-based
  local-gateway: 172.16.2.1:0 (static)
  remote-gateway: 172.16.3.1:0 (static)
  mode: ike-v1
  interface: 'port2' (4)
  rx  packets: 8  bytes: 960  errors: 0
  tx  packets: 8  bytes: 480  errors: 52
  dpd: on-demand/negotiated  idle: 20000ms  retry: 3  count: 0
  selectors
     name: 'VPNtoSite2'
     auto-negotiate: disable
     mode: tunnel
     src: 0:10.0.1.0/255.255.255.0:0
     dst: 0:10.0.2.0/255.255.255.0:0
     SA
       lifetime/rekey: 43200/42789
       mtu: 1438
       tx-esp-seq: 9
       replay: enabled
       inbound
         spi: ece57217
         enc:  aes-cb   7747288ff924a97c8754b3ff2c72837f
         auth:    sha1  9be4eac54d718c03e24f013158a3087f5b564d5d
       outbound
```

```
        spi: 9468e952

        enc:    aes-cb   44dccd823b56730473ed296fdf4f6433

        auth:   sha1    f5d87b7372d179a357d28469e38fb915a147f1d0


FG-A #
```

Example 4.14

```
FG-A # get vpn ike gateway


vd: root/0   <- VDOM name

name: VPNtoSite2

version: 1

interface: port2 4

addr: 172.16.2.1:500 -> 172.16.3.1:500 <- peer IPs

created: 214s ago

IKE SA  created: 2/2  established: 2/2  time: 0/10520/21040 ms

IPsec SA  created: 1/1  established: 1/1  time: 0/0/0 ms


  id/spi: 7  f1d8ca6090b7d820/8363512edae52f5d

  direction: responder

  status: established 196-196s ago = 0ms

  proposal: aes-256-sha1

  key: 4be504c31e1d0928-8102a051492a07c6-b675e85229ef2bb0-4c9f618bd9e7053f

  lifetime/rekey: 86400/85933

  DPD sent/recv: 00000000/00000000


  id/spi: 4  65482aeeb7cb95ce/dcdb0f7817f1edd6

  direction: initiator

  status: established 214-193s ago = 21040ms
```

```
    proposal: aes-256-sha1

    key: 865179f9b28494aa-1929b66e41e337bb-fdfa4dbc0de298ca-21dbe27b2cfbc310

    lifetime/rekey: 86400/85906

    DPD sent/recv: 00000000/00000000


FG-A #
```

By checking **get vpn ipsec stats crypto** you can verify which encryption and integrity protocols are used in your IPsec tunnels:

Example 4.15

```
FG-A # get vpn ipsec stats crypto
IPsec crypto devices in use:
SOFTWARE:
    Encryption (encrypted/decrypted)
        null            : 0                 0
        des             : 0                 0
        3des            : 0                 0
        aes-cbc         : 105               105
        aes-gcm         : 0                 0
        aria            : 0                 0
        seed            : 0                 0
        chacha20poly1305: 0                 0
    Integrity (generated/validated)
        null            : 0                 0
        md5             : 0                 0
        sha1            : 105               105
        sha256          : 0                 0
        sha384          : 0                 0
```

```
        sha512    : 0                  0
```

In the next example you see a summary of all VPN tunnels. You can view also which tunnel is up or down, and what is the number of packets received, sent, and the number of errors:

Example 4.16

```
FG-A # get vpn ipsec tunnel summary
'VPNtoSite2' 172.16.3.1:0  selectors(total,up): 1/1  rx(pkt,err): 148/0  tx(pkt,err): 148/58


FG-A #
```

4.1.2 Example #2 – pre-share secret mismatch

Let's analyze the case with two different pre-shared secrets set on the VPN peers.

I use the same diagnose commands in all IPsec examples:

Example 4.17

```
diagnose debug application ike 255
diagnose debug enable
```

During the negotiation, after 3rd message (in main mode), there is an error:

Example 4.18

```
ike 0:VPNtoSite2:5: responder: main mode get 3rd message...

ike 0:VPNtoSite2:5: dec
8D33C208E4180CC186CF5460271284BE05100201000000000000006C374EF1D9EB7FD496DF3ACBB4BF7BEED6E96C
72B91D5E2F00793A486009143DA1DF74B00E76A4B6A9079BEE32F71C3CC4028BDADAFD9EFAEB8722D68D5BD4347D
935036359C23CD829525FF3997C0017A

ike 0:VPNtoSite2:5: parse error
```

```
ike 0:VPNtoSite2:5: probable pre-shared secret mismatch
ike 0:VPNtoSite2:5: out
```

The same error message is on the second VPN peer:

Example 4.19

```
ike 0:VPNtoSite1:5: responder: main mode get 3rd message...
ike 0:VPNtoSite1:5: dec
8CAE2CD4115F8D82516EFFDABD6910FE05100201000000000000006C35B80DD5E26EA651BE8BD4669FFBC18FF0F9
C6C2762ECA947051DF4855C52DB79E4C9B3946284C640AF321490B514CF3762A30A7FCD174F405FC040AA81840A9
BEBB109CC81D99CD3DBDA039D7999AD4
ike 0:VPNtoSite1:5: parse error
ike 0:VPNtoSite1:5: probable pre-shared secret mismatch
ike 0:VPNtoSite1:5: out
```

4.1.3 Example #3 – phase1 mismatch settings (authentication, encryption)

You can define many Phase 1 proposals, but at least one should match the settings on the second VPN peer. In the below output, there are a couple of incoming proposals from the remote peer. They have different encryption and authentication algorithms and Diffie-Hellman groups:

Example 4.20

```
ike 0:8caa9bb556788b3e/0000000000000000:18: incoming proposal:
ike 0:8caa9bb556788b3e/0000000000000000:18: proposal id = 0:
ike 0:8caa9bb556788b3e/0000000000000000:18:   protocol id = ISAKMP:
ike 0:8caa9bb556788b3e/0000000000000000:18:     trans_id = KEY_IKE.
ike 0:8caa9bb556788b3e/0000000000000000:18:     encapsulation = IKE/none
ike 0:8caa9bb556788b3e/0000000000000000:18:       type=OAKLEY_ENCRYPT_ALG, val=AES_CBC, key-len=128
```

```
ike 0:8caa9bb556788b3e/0000000000000000:18:          type=OAKLEY_HASH_ALG, val=SHA2_256.
ike 0:8caa9bb556788b3e/0000000000000000:18:          type=AUTH_METHOD, val=PRESHARED_KEY.
ike 0:8caa9bb556788b3e/0000000000000000:18:          type=OAKLEY_GROUP, val=MODP2048.
ike 0:8caa9bb556788b3e/0000000000000000:18: ISAKMP SA lifetime=86400
ike 0:8caa9bb556788b3e/0000000000000000:18: proposal id = 0:
ike 0:8caa9bb556788b3e/0000000000000000:18:    protocol id = ISAKMP:
ike 0:8caa9bb556788b3e/0000000000000000:18:      trans_id = KEY_IKE.
ike 0:8caa9bb556788b3e/0000000000000000:18:      encapsulation = IKE/none
ike 0:8caa9bb556788b3e/0000000000000000:18:          type=OAKLEY_ENCRYPT_ALG, val=AES_CBC, key-len=128
ike 0:8caa9bb556788b3e/0000000000000000:18:          type=OAKLEY_HASH_ALG, val=SHA2_256.
ike 0:8caa9bb556788b3e/0000000000000000:18:          type=AUTH_METHOD, val=PRESHARED_KEY.
ike 0:8caa9bb556788b3e/0000000000000000:18:          type=OAKLEY_GROUP, val=MODP1536.
ike 0:8caa9bb556788b3e/0000000000000000:18: ISAKMP SA lifetime=86400
ike 0:8caa9bb556788b3e/0000000000000000:18: proposal id = 0:
ike 0:8caa9bb556788b3e/0000000000000000:18:    protocol id = ISAKMP:
ike 0:8caa9bb556788b3e/0000000000000000:18:      trans_id = KEY_IKE.
ike 0:8caa9bb556788b3e/0000000000000000:18:      encapsulation = IKE/none
ike 0:8caa9bb556788b3e/0000000000000000:18:          type=OAKLEY_ENCRYPT_ALG, val=AES_CBC, key-len=256
ike 0:8caa9bb556788b3e/0000000000000000:18:          type=OAKLEY_HASH_ALG, val=SHA2_256.
ike 0:8caa9bb556788b3e/0000000000000000:18:          type=AUTH_METHOD, val=PRESHARED_KEY.
ike 0:8caa9bb556788b3e/0000000000000000:18:          type=OAKLEY_GROUP, val=MODP2048.
ike 0:8caa9bb556788b3e/0000000000000000:18: ISAKMP SA lifetime=86400
ike 0:8caa9bb556788b3e/0000000000000000:18: proposal id = 0:
ike 0:8caa9bb556788b3e/0000000000000000:18:    protocol id = ISAKMP:
ike 0:8caa9bb556788b3e/0000000000000000:18:      trans_id = KEY_IKE.
ike 0:8caa9bb556788b3e/0000000000000000:18:      encapsulation = IKE/none
ike 0:8caa9bb556788b3e/0000000000000000:18:          type=OAKLEY_ENCRYPT_ALG, val=AES_CBC, key-len=256
ike 0:8caa9bb556788b3e/0000000000000000:18:          type=OAKLEY_HASH_ALG, val=SHA2_256.
```

ike 0:8caa9bb556788b3e/0000000000000000:18:   type=AUTH_METHOD, val=PRESHARED_KEY.

ike 0:8caa9bb556788b3e/0000000000000000:18:   type=OAKLEY_GROUP, val=MODP1536.

ike 0:8caa9bb556788b3e/0000000000000000:18: ISAKMP SA lifetime=86400

ike 0:8caa9bb556788b3e/0000000000000000:18: proposal id = 0:

ike 0:8caa9bb556788b3e/0000000000000000:18:   protocol id = ISAKMP:

ike 0:8caa9bb556788b3e/0000000000000000:18:   trans_id = KEY_IKE.

ike 0:8caa9bb556788b3e/0000000000000000:18:   encapsulation = IKE/none

ike 0:8caa9bb556788b3e/0000000000000000:18:   type=OAKLEY_ENCRYPT_ALG, val=AES_CBC, key-len=128

ike 0:8caa9bb556788b3e/0000000000000000:18:   type=OAKLEY_HASH_ALG, val=SHA.

ike 0:8caa9bb556788b3e/0000000000000000:18:   type=AUTH_METHOD, val=PRESHARED_KEY.

ike 0:8caa9bb556788b3e/0000000000000000:18:   type=OAKLEY_GROUP, val=MODP2048.

ike 0:8caa9bb556788b3e/0000000000000000:18: ISAKMP SA lifetime=86400

ike 0:8caa9bb556788b3e/0000000000000000:18: proposal id = 0:

ike 0:8caa9bb556788b3e/0000000000000000:18:   protocol id = ISAKMP:

ike 0:8caa9bb556788b3e/0000000000000000:18:   trans_id = KEY_IKE.

ike 0:8caa9bb556788b3e/0000000000000000:18:   encapsulation = IKE/none

ike 0:8caa9bb556788b3e/0000000000000000:18:   type=OAKLEY_ENCRYPT_ALG, val=AES_CBC, key-len=128

ike 0:8caa9bb556788b3e/0000000000000000:18:   type=OAKLEY_HASH_ALG, val=SHA.

ike 0:8caa9bb556788b3e/0000000000000000:18:   type=AUTH_METHOD, val=PRESHARED_KEY.

ike 0:8caa9bb556788b3e/0000000000000000:18:   type=OAKLEY_GROUP, val=MODP1536.

ike 0:8caa9bb556788b3e/0000000000000000:18: ISAKMP SA lifetime=86400

ike 0:8caa9bb556788b3e/0000000000000000:18: proposal id = 0:

ike 0:8caa9bb556788b3e/0000000000000000:18:   protocol id = ISAKMP:

ike 0:8caa9bb556788b3e/0000000000000000:18:   trans_id = KEY_IKE.

ike 0:8caa9bb556788b3e/0000000000000000:18:   encapsulation = IKE/none

ike 0:8caa9bb556788b3e/0000000000000000:18:   type=OAKLEY_ENCRYPT_ALG, val=AES_CBC, key-len=256

ike 0:8caa9bb556788b3e/0000000000000000:18:   type=OAKLEY_HASH_ALG, val=SHA.

ike 0:8caa9bb556788b3e/0000000000000000:18:   type=AUTH_METHOD, val=PRESHARED_KEY.

```
ike 0:8caa9bb556788b3e/0000000000000000:18:         type=OAKLEY_GROUP, val=MODP2048.
ike 0:8caa9bb556788b3e/0000000000000000:18: ISAKMP SA lifetime=86400
ike 0:8caa9bb556788b3e/0000000000000000:18: proposal id = 0:
ike 0:8caa9bb556788b3e/0000000000000000:18:   protocol id = ISAKMP:
ike 0:8caa9bb556788b3e/0000000000000000:18:     trans_id = KEY_IKE.
ike 0:8caa9bb556788b3e/0000000000000000:18:     encapsulation = IKE/none
ike 0:8caa9bb556788b3e/0000000000000000:18:        type=OAKLEY_ENCRYPT_ALG, val=AES_CBC, key-len=256
ike 0:8caa9bb556788b3e/0000000000000000:18:        type=OAKLEY_HASH_ALG, val=SHA.
ike 0:8caa9bb556788b3e/0000000000000000:18:        type=AUTH_METHOD, val=PRESHARED_KEY.
ike 0:8caa9bb556788b3e/0000000000000000:18:        type=OAKLEY_GROUP, val=MODP1536.
ike 0:8caa9bb556788b3e/0000000000000000:18: ISAKMP SA lifetime=86400
```

There are only two proposals on the local device:

Example 4.21

```
ike 0:8caa9bb556788b3e/0000000000000000:18: my proposal, gw VPNtoSite2:
ike 0:8caa9bb556788b3e/0000000000000000:18: proposal id = 1:
ike 0:8caa9bb556788b3e/0000000000000000:18:   protocol id = ISAKMP:
ike 0:8caa9bb556788b3e/0000000000000000:18:     trans_id = KEY_IKE.
ike 0:8caa9bb556788b3e/0000000000000000:18:     encapsulation = IKE/none
ike 0:8caa9bb556788b3e/0000000000000000:18:        type=OAKLEY_ENCRYPT_ALG, val=3DES_CBC.
ike 0:8caa9bb556788b3e/0000000000000000:18:        type=OAKLEY_HASH_ALG, val=SHA.
ike 0:8caa9bb556788b3e/0000000000000000:18:        type=AUTH_METHOD, val=PRESHARED_KEY.
ike 0:8caa9bb556788b3e/0000000000000000:18:        type=OAKLEY_GROUP, val=ECP256BP.
ike 0:8caa9bb556788b3e/0000000000000000:18: ISAKMP SA lifetime=86400
ike 0:8caa9bb556788b3e/0000000000000000:18: proposal id = 1:
ike 0:8caa9bb556788b3e/0000000000000000:18:   protocol id = ISAKMP:
ike 0:8caa9bb556788b3e/0000000000000000:18:     trans_id = KEY_IKE.
```

```
ike 0:8caa9bb556788b3e/0000000000000000:18:         encapsulation = IKE/none
ike 0:8caa9bb556788b3e/0000000000000000:18:             type=OAKLEY_ENCRYPT_ALG, val=3DES_CBC.
ike 0:8caa9bb556788b3e/0000000000000000:18:             type=OAKLEY_HASH_ALG, val=SHA.
ike 0:8caa9bb556788b3e/0000000000000000:18:             type=AUTH_METHOD, val=PRESHARED_KEY.
ike 0:8caa9bb556788b3e/0000000000000000:18:             type=OAKLEY_GROUP, val=MODP1024.
ike 0:8caa9bb556788b3e/0000000000000000:18: ISAKMP SA lifetime=86400
```

but the negotiation fails because there are no matching proposals:

Example 4.22

```
ike 0:8caa9bb556788b3e/0000000000000000:18: negotiation failure
ike Negotiate ISAKMP SA Error: ike 0:8caa9bb556788b3e/0000000000000000:18: no SA proposal chosen
ike 0:VPNtoSite2:16: out
```

On the remote peer you can spot the same error:

Example 4.23

```
ike 0:3b98b3df3773badd/0000000000000000:11: negotiation failure
ike Negotiate ISAKMP SA Error: ike 0:3b98b3df3773badd/0000000000000000:11: no SA proposal chosen
```

4.1.4 Example #4 – phase2 mismatch settings (selectors)

In the next case the phase2 settings are different with no matching selectors. In some cases, the same error messages on both peers are not the same. It is important to have access to diagnose outputs from both devices.

In the below output there is no information about the reason why the tunnel is down. There are many retransmissions and the final negotiation failure due to the timeout:

Example 4.24

```
ike 0:VPNtoSite2:2:VPNtoSite2:0: initiator selectors 0 0:10.0.1.0/255.255.255.0:0:0-
>0:10.0.0.0/255.255.0.0:0:0

...

ike 0:VPNtoSite2:2: sent IKE msg (quick_i1send): 172.16.2.1:500->172.16.3.1:500, len=604,
id=9e6ada64545c397c/96ab648c446fa614:fd0a04e2

ike 0:VPNtoSite2:2: out

...

ike 0:VPNtoSite2:2: sent IKE msg (P2_RETRANSMIT): 172.16.2.1:500->172.16.3.1:500, len=604,
id=9e6ada64545c397c/96ab648c446fa614:fd0a04e2

ike 0:VPNtoSite2:VPNtoSite2: IPsec SA connect 4 172.16.2.1->172.16.3.1:0

ike 0:VPNtoSite2:VPNtoSite2: using existing connection

ike 0:VPNtoSite2:VPNtoSite2: config found

ike 0:VPNtoSite2: request is on the queue

ike 0:VPNtoSite2:2: out

...

ike 0:VPNtoSite2:2: sent IKE msg (P2_RETRANSMIT): 172.16.2.1:500->172.16.3.1:500, len=604,
id=9e6ada64545c397c/96ab648c446fa614:fd0a04e2

ike 0:VPNtoSite2:VPNtoSite2: IPsec SA connect 4 172.16.2.1->172.16.3.1:0

ike 0:VPNtoSite2:VPNtoSite2: using existing connection

ike 0:VPNtoSite2:VPNtoSite2: config found

ike 0:VPNtoSite2: request is on the queue

ike shrank heap by 155648 bytes

ike 0:VPNtoSite2:2: out

...

ike 0:VPNtoSite2:2: sent IKE msg (P2_RETRANSMIT): 172.16.2.1:500->172.16.3.1:500, len=604,
id=9e6ada64545c397c/96ab648c446fa614:fd0a04e2

ike 0:VPNtoSite2:VPNtoSite2: IPsec SA connect 4 172.16.2.1->172.16.3.1:0

ike 0:VPNtoSite2:VPNtoSite2: using existing connection

ike 0:VPNtoSite2:VPNtoSite2: config found

ike 0:VPNtoSite2: request is on the queue
```

```
ike 0:VPNtoSite2:VPNtoSite2: IPsec SA connect 4 172.16.2.1->172.16.3.1:0
ike 0:VPNtoSite2:VPNtoSite2: using existing connection
ike 0:VPNtoSite2:VPNtoSite2: config found
ike 0:VPNtoSite2: request is on the queue
ike 0:VPNtoSite2:VPNtoSite2: IPsec SA connect 4 172.16.2.1->172.16.3.1:0
ike 0:VPNtoSite2:VPNtoSite2: using existing connection
ike 0:VPNtoSite2:VPNtoSite2: config found
ike 0:VPNtoSite2: request is on the queue
ike 0:VPNtoSite2:VPNtoSite2: IPsec SA connect 4 172.16.2.1->172.16.3.1:0
ike 0:VPNtoSite2:VPNtoSite2: using existing connection
ike 0:VPNtoSite2:VPNtoSite2: config found
ike 0:VPNtoSite2: request is on the queue
ike 0:VPNtoSite2:2: out
...
ike 0:VPNtoSite2:2:VPNtoSite2:0: quick-mode negotiation failed due to retry timeout
ike 0:VPNtoSite2:2: send IKE SA delete 9e6ada64545c397c/96ab648c446fa614
...
ike 0:VPNtoSite2:2: sent IKE msg (ISAKMP SA DELETE-NOTIFY): 172.16.2.1:500->172.16.3.1:500, len=92,
```

On the remote device the situation is clear. There are no matching phase2 settings:

Example 4.25

```
ike 0:VPNtoSite1:0:0: peer proposal is: peer:0:10.0.1.0-10.0.1.255:0, me:0:10.0.0.0-10.0.255.255:0
ike 0:VPNtoSite1:0:VPNtoSite1:0: trying
ike 0:VPNtoSite1:0:0: specified selectors mismatch
ike 0:VPNtoSite1:0:0: peer: type=7/7, local=0:10.0.0.0-10.0.255.255:0, remote=0:10.0.1.0-10.0.1.255:0
ike 0:VPNtoSite1:0:0: mine: type=7/7, local=0:10.0.2.0-10.0.2.255:0, remote=0:10.0.1.0-10.0.1.255:0
```

```
ike 0:VPNtoSite1:0:0: no matching phase2 found
ike 0:VPNtoSite1:0:0: failed to get responder proposal
ike 0:VPNtoSite1:0: error processing quick-mode message from 172.16.2.1 as responder
```

4.1.5   Example #5 – mismatch IKE mode (aggressive vs main mode)

In the next example we have two peers in different modes: aggressive and main mode. From the debug output you can see that the initiator and responder send messages in different modes. There is no clear error message saying the problem might be different IKE modes. You should already know they are incompatible.

Example 4.26

```
ike 0:VPNtoSite2: created connection: 0xac23f90 4 172.16.2.1->172.16.3.1:500.

ike 0:VPNtoSite2:73: initiator: aggressive mode is sending 1st message...

ike 0:VPNtoSite2:73: cookie ca47838269cffba8/0000000000000000

ike 0:VPNtoSite2:73: out

...

ike 0:6f34831743d2e87d/0000000000000000:74: responder: main mode get 1st message...

ike 0:6f34831743d2e87d/0000000000000000:74: VID RFC 3947 4A131C81070358455C5728F20E95452F

ike 0:6f34831743d2e87d/0000000000000000:74: VID draft-ietf-ipsec-nat-t-ike-03 7D9419A65310CA6F2C179D9215529D56

ike 0:6f34831743d2e87d/0000000000000000:74: VID draft-ietf-ipsec-nat-t-ike-02 CD60464335DF21F87CFDB2FC68B6A448

ike 0:6f34831743d2e87d/0000000000000000:74: VID draft-ietf-ipsec-nat-t-ike-02\n 90CB80913EBB696E086381B5EC427B1F

ike 0:6f34831743d2e87d/0000000000000000:74: VID draft-ietf-ipsec-nat-t-ike-01 16F6CA16E4A4066D83821A0F0AEAA862

ike 0:6f34831743d2e87d/0000000000000000:74: VID draft-ietf-ipsec-nat-t-ike-00 4485152D18B6BBCD0BE8A8469579DDCC

ike 0:6f34831743d2e87d/0000000000000000:74: VID DPD AFCAD71368A1F1C96B8696FC77570100

ike 0:6f34831743d2e87d/0000000000000000:74: VID FRAGMENTATION 4048B7D56EBCE88525E7DE7F00D6C2D3
```

```
ike 0:6f34831743d2e87d/0000000000000000:74: VID FRAGMENTATION
4048B7D56EBCE88525E7DE7F00D6C2D3C0000000

ike 0:6f34831743d2e87d/0000000000000000:74: VID FORTIGATE 8299031757A36082C6A621DE00000000

ike 0:6f34831743d2e87d/0000000000000000:74: incoming proposal:

ike 0:6f34831743d2e87d/0000000000000000:74: proposal id = 0:

ike 0:6f34831743d2e87d/0000000000000000:74:    protocol id = ISAKMP:

ike 0:6f34831743d2e87d/0000000000000000:74:       trans_id = KEY_IKE.

ike 0:6f34831743d2e87d/0000000000000000:74:       encapsulation = IKE/none

ike 0:6f34831743d2e87d/0000000000000000:74:          type=OAKLEY_ENCRYPT_ALG, val=AES_CBC, key-len=128

ike 0:6f34831743d2e87d/0000000000000000:74:          type=OAKLEY_HASH_ALG, val=SHA2_256.

ike 0:6f34831743d2e87d/0000000000000000:74:          type=AUTH_METHOD, val=PRESHARED_KEY.

ike 0:6f34831743d2e87d/0000000000000000:74:          type=OAKLEY_GROUP, val=MODP2048.

ike 0:6f34831743d2e87d/0000000000000000:74: ISAKMP SA lifetime=86400

...

ike 0:6f34831743d2e87d/0000000000000000:74: negotiation failure

ike Negotiate ISAKMP SA Error: ike 0:6f34831743d2e87d/0000000000000000:74: no SA proposal chosen

ike 0:VPNtoSite2:73: out

...

ike 0:6eb68188e496a23e/0000000000000000:77: negotiation failure

ike Negotiate ISAKMP SA Error: ike 0:6eb68188e496a23e/0000000000000000:77: no SA proposal chosen

ike 0:VPNtoSite2:73: negotiation timeout, deleting

ike 0:VPNtoSite2: connection expiring due to phase1 down

ike 0:VPNtoSite2: deleting

ike 0:VPNtoSite2: deleted
```

On the remote peer there is pretty much the same information presented:

Example 4.27

```
ike 0: IKEv1 exchange=Aggressive id=6073e68743de1d8d/0000000000000000 len=600
ike 0: in
...
ike 0:6073e68743de1d8d/0000000000000000:72: responder: aggressive mode get 1st message...
...
ike 0::72: peer identifier IPV4_ADDR 172.16.2.1
ike 0: IKEv1 Aggressive, comes 172.16.2.1:500->172.16.3.1 6
...
ike 0:6073e68743de1d8d/0000000000000000:72: negotiation failure
ike Negotiate ISAKMP SA Error: ike 0:6073e68743de1d8d/0000000000000000:72: no SA proposal chosen
ike 0:VPNtoSite1:68: negotiation timeout, deleting
ike 0:VPNtoSite1: connection expiring due to phase1 down
ike 0:VPNtoSite1: deleting
ike 0:VPNtoSite1: deleted
```

As you probably noticed the error "no SA proposal chosen" is the same, when you have no matching proposals as shown in #3. The main difference is the message about modes, which should help you to figure out what the issue is.

4.1.6   Example #6 – mismatch IKE versions (IKEv1 vs IKEv2)

In the last case we have the local peer with IKEv1 and the remote with IKEv2. There is no combability between them and they cannot "understand" each other. As you can see below there is no error message with any useful explanation. There are different IKE versions, but you need to check the debug output from both VPN peers to spot it.

On the first peer, you can see IKEv1 exchange and information about the 'main mode'. You should notice it is IKEv1 since there is no main and aggressive in IKEv2:

Example 4.28

```
ike 0: comes 172.16.3.1:500->172.16.2.1:500,ifindex=4....
ike 0: IKEv1 exchange=Identity Protection id=f011e9c959d3700d/0000000000000000 len=572
...
ike 0:f011e9c959d3700d/0000000000000000:18: responder: main mode get 1st message...
...
ike 0:f011e9c959d3700d/0000000000000000:18: negotiation failure
ike Negotiate ISAKMP SA Error: ike 0:f011e9c959d3700d/0000000000000000:18: no SA proposal chosen
...
ike 0:675cd875521d8142/0000000000000000:20: responder: main mode get 1st message...
...
ike 0:675cd875521d8142/0000000000000000:20: negotiation failure
ike Negotiate ISAKMP SA Error: ike 0:675cd875521d8142/0000000000000000:20: no SA proposal chosen
```

On the second peer there is IKEv2, which is incompatible with IKEv1:

Example 4.29

```
ike 0: comes 172.16.2.1:500->172.16.3.1:500,ifindex=6....
ike 0: IKEv2 exchange=SA_INIT id=34749d2fbdbbd41c/0000000000000000 len=632
...
ike 0:34749d2fbdbbd41c/0000000000000000:21: incoming proposal:
ike 0:34749d2fbdbbd41c/0000000000000000:21: proposal id = 1:
ike 0:34749d2fbdbbd41c/0000000000000000:21:     protocol = IKEv2:
ike 0:34749d2fbdbbd41c/0000000000000000:21:        encapsulation = IKEv2/none
ike 0:34749d2fbdbbd41c/0000000000000000:21:           type=ENCR, val=AES_CBC (key_len = 128)
ike 0:34749d2fbdbbd41c/0000000000000000:21:           type=INTEGR, val=AUTH_HMAC_SHA2_256_128
ike 0:34749d2fbdbbd41c/0000000000000000:21:           type=PRF, val=PRF_HMAC_SHA2_256
ike 0:34749d2fbdbbd41c/0000000000000000:21:           type=DH_GROUP, val=MODP2048.
```

```
ike 0:34749d2fbdbbd41c/0000000000000000:21:          type=DH_GROUP, val=MODP1536.
...
ike 0:34749d2fbdbbd41c/0000000000000000:23: no proposal chosen
ike Negotiate SA Error: ike ike  [10132]
ike 0:VPNtoSite1:19: negotiation timeout, deleting
ike 0:VPNtoSite1: connection expiring due to phase1 down
ike 0:VPNtoSite1: deleting
ike 0:VPNtoSite1: deleted
```

4.2 SSL-VPN

SSL VPN is more popular than IPsec for remote access. There are two deployment modes: web and tunnel mode. For the first one we need Internet browser as a client. In tunnel mode we need FortiClient installed on the user's computer. In next few examples I present the debug output for a functional and working SSL VPN. Then, I show ones with configuration errors.

4.2.1 Example #1 – web-based mode

In this case the configuration is correct, and the user can establish the SSL VPN tunnel using web-based mode.

Example 4.30

```
diagnose debug application sslvpn 255
diagnose debug enable
```

In the following debug output you see: the TTL version, the cipher suite, the username and group membership.

Example 4.31

```
[463:root:70]allocSSLConn:281 sconn 0x7f66bda35800 (0:root)

[463:root:70]client cert requirement: no

…

[463:root:70]SSL established: TLSv1.3 TLS_AES_256_GCM_SHA384 <- TLS version and cipher suite

[463:root:70]rmt_web_auth_info_parser_common:441 no session id in auth info

[463:root:70]rmt_web_get_access_cache:758 invalid cache, ret=4103

[463:root:71]allocSSLConn:281 sconn 0x7f66bda39800 (0:root)

…

[463:root:72]sslConnGotoNextState:300 error (last state: 1, closeOp: 0)

[463:root:72]Destroy sconn 0x7f66bda3bc00, connSize=2. (root)

[463:root:70]epollAddPending:528

read : needed: 0 ((nil)) evRead  0x4 ev 0x1 (0)

write: needed: 1 (0x135ce40) evWrite 0x4 ev 0x1 (0)

[463:root:70]epollFdHandler:643 s: 0x7f66bda35800 event: 0x14

[463:root:70]Destroy sconn 0x7f66bda35800, connSize=1. (root)

[463:root:71]sslConnGotoNextState:300 error (last state: 1, closeOp: 0)

[463:root:71]Destroy sconn 0x7f66bda39800, connSize=0. (root)

[463:root:73]allocSSLConn:281 sconn 0x7f66bda35800 (0:root)

[463:root:73]client cert requirement: no

…

[463:root:73]SSL established: TLSv1.3 TLS_AES_256_GCM_SHA384

[463:root:73]rmt_web_auth_info_parser_common:441 no session id in auth info

[463:root:73]rmt_web_access_check:684 access failed, uri=[/remote/logincheck],ret=4103,

[463:root:73]rmt_logincheck_cb_handler:921 user 'userA' has a matched local entry. <- username

[463:root:73]two factor check for userA: off <- two factor authentication is off

[463:root:73]fam_auth_send_req:576 with server blacklist:

[463:root:73]SSL VPN login matched rule (0).
```

```
[463:root:73]rmt_web_session_create:709 create web session, idx[0]

[463:root:73]deconstruct_session_id:378 decode session id ok,    <- session details
user=[userA],group=[SSL_VPN_USERS],authserver=[],portal=[web-
access],host=[172.16.3.1],realm=[],idx=0,auth=1,sid=726d8e41, login=1585773900,
access=1585773900

…

[463:root:74]allocSSLConn:281 sconn 0x7f66bda3ac00 (0:root)
```

4.2.2 Example #2 – tunnel-based mode

Below you can see the **debug diagnose application sslvpn** output of tunnel mode SSL VPN with no configuration errors:

Example 4.32

```
[463:root:52]deconstruct_session_id:378 decode session id ok, <- tunnel mode
user=[userA],group=[SSL_VPN_USERS],authserver=[],portal=[full-
access],host=[172.16.3.1],realm=[],idx=0,auth=1,sid=1927e8ed, login=1585771465,
access=1585771465

…

[463:root:52]form_ipv4_split_tunnel_addr:1544 Matched policy (id = 2) to add split tunnel
routing address

…

…:52]sslvpn_reserve_dynip:1157 tunnel vd[root] ip[10.212.134.200] app session idx[0] <- IP
allocation

[463:root:52]form_ipv4_split_tunnel_addr:1544 Matched policy (id = 2) to add split tunnel
routing address

[463:root:53]allocSSLConn:281 sconn 0x7f66bda37400 (0:root)

[463:root:53]client cert requirement: no

[463:root:53]SSL established: TLSv1.2 ECDHE-RSA-AES256-GCM-SHA384 <- TLS version and cipher
suite

…

[463:root:53]sslvpn_tunnel_handler,48, Calling rmt_conn_access_ex.

…
```

```
[463:root:53]sslvpn_tunnel_handler,146, Calling tunnel.

[463:root:53]tunnelEnter:416 0x7f66bda37400:0x7f66bdb8c000 sslvpn user[userA],type
1,logintime 0 vd 0

[463:root:53]sconn 0x7f66bda37400 (0:root) vfid=0 local=[172.16.1.1] remote=[172.16.3.1]
dynamicip=[10.212.134.200]   <- local and remote public IPs, and dynamic IP assigned for the
user

[463:root:53]Prepare to launch ppp service...

[463:root:53]tun: ppp 0x7f66bdb90000 dev (ssl.root) opened fd 36

[463:root:53]Will add auth policy for policy 2 for user userA:SSL_VPN_USERS

[463:root:53]Add auth logon for user userA:SSL_VPN_USERS, matched group number 1

[463:root:0]RCV: LCP Configure_Request id(1) len(14) [Maximum_Received_Unit 1354]
[Magic_Number FE007610]

[463:root:0]SND: LCP Configure_Request id(1) len(10) [Magic_Number F24278FB]

[463:root:0]lcp_reqci: returning CONFACK.

[463:root:0]SND: LCP Configure_Ack id(1) len(14) [Maximum_Received_Unit 1354] [Magic_Number
FE007610]

[463:root:0]RCV: LCP Configure_Ack id(1) len(10) [Magic_Number F24278FB]

[463:root:0]lcp_up: with mtu 1354 <- MTU

[463:root:0]SND: IPCP Configure_Request id(1) [IP_Address 172.16.1.1]

[463:root:0]RCV: IPCP Configure_Request id(0) [IP_Address 0.0.0.0] [Primary_DNS_IP_Address
0.0.0.0] [Secondary_DNS_IP_Address 0.0.0.0]

[463:root:0]ipcp: returning Configure-NAK

[463:root:0]SND: IPCP Configure_Nak id(0) [IP_Address 10.212.134.200]
[Primary_DNS_IP_Address 192.168.153.1] [Secondary_DNS_IP_Address 10.0.2.254]   <- DNS settings

[463:root:0]RCV: IPCP Configure_Ack id(1) [IP_Address 172.16.1.1]

[463:root:0]RCV: IPCP Configure_Request id(1) [IP_Address 10.212.134.200]
[Primary_DNS_IP_Address 192.168.153.1] [Secondary_DNS_IP_Address 10.0.2.254]

[463:root:0]ipcp: returning Configure-ACK

[463:root:0]SND: IPCP Configure_Ack id(1) [IP_Address 10.212.134.200]
[Primary_DNS_IP_Address 192.168.153.1] [Secondary_DNS_IP_Address 10.0.2.254]

[463:root:0]ipcp: up ppp:0x7f66bdb90000 caller:0x7f66bda37400 tun:36

[463:root:0]Cannot determine ethernet address for proxy ARP

[463:root:0]local IP address 172.16.1.1 <- local IP of the gateway
```

```
[463:root:0]remote IP address 10.212.134.200 <- the dynamic IP assigned for the user
[463:root:53]sslvpn_ppp_associate_fd_to_ipaddr:279 associate 10.212.134.200 to tun
(ssl.root:36)
[463:root:52]sslvpn_read_request_common,639, ret=-1 error=-1, sconn=0x7f66bda35800.
[463:root:52]Destroy sconn 0x7f66bda35800, connSize=1. (root)
```

4.2.3 Example #3 – invalid user

In case the user is not permitted to access the SSL VPN, the following error message appears:

Example 4.33

```
[463:root:7]login_failed:272 user[admin],auth_type=0 failed [sslvpn_login_unknown_user]
```

For the user 'admin' in **diagnose debug flow** output there is no matching firewall policy:

Example 4.34

```
diagnose debug flow filter addr 172.16.3.1
diagnose debug flow show function-name enable
diagnose debug flow show iprope enable
diagnose debug flow trace start 100
diagnose debug enable
```

Example 4.35

```
id=20085 trace_id=10 func=print_pkt_detail line=5517 msg="vd-root:0 received a
packet(proto=6, 172.16.3.1:51683->172.16.1.1:10443) from port1. flag [S], seq 1262106172,
ack 0, win 8192"

id=20085 trace_id=10 func=init_ip_session_common line=5682 msg="allocate a new session-
00002811"
```

```
id=20085 trace_id=10 func=vf_ip_route_input_common line=2591 msg="find a route:
flag=80000000 gw-172.16.1.1 via root"

id=20085 trace_id=10 func=fw_local_in_handler line=410 msg="iprope_in_check() check failed
on policy 0, drop"
```

4.2.4 Example #4 – user not permitted to web-based mode

When the user is permitted to use the tunnel-based SSL VPN, he/she can still access the web portal. On the main page it will be stated that the web-based mode is denied. The user can only download FortiClient from the portal.

4.2.5 Example #5 – user not permitted to tunnel mode

You may have users which are permitted to web-based SSL VPN, but without access to the client mode (tunnel). They see the following error when they try to connect with the FortiClient:

Figure 4.1

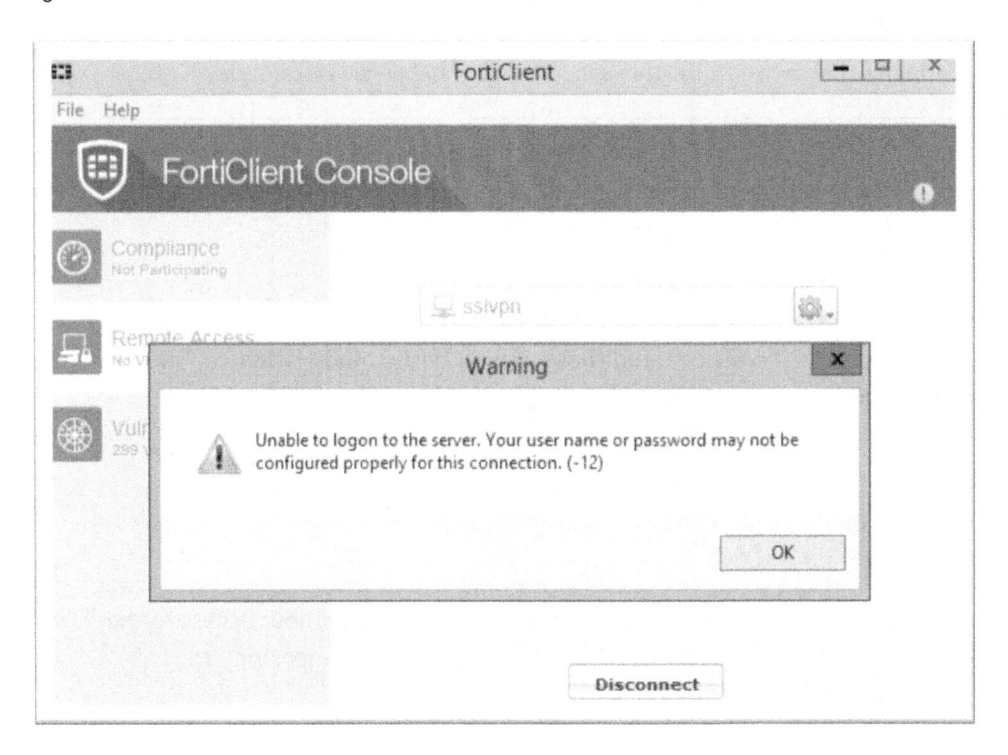

![FortiClient Console warning: Unable to logon to the server. Your user name or password may not be configured properly for this connection. (-12)]

In this case you can find more information on the client. The FortiGate is just showing "timeout" error:

Example 4.36

```
[463:root:56]Timeout for connection 0x7f66bda35800.

[463:root:56]Destroy sconn 0x7f66bda35800, connSize=0. (root)

[463:root:0]sslvpn_internal_remove_one_web_session:2711 web session
(root:userA:SSL_VPN_USERS:172.16.3.1:0 1) removed for tunnel connection setup timeout for
SSLVPN Client
```

5 Routing

FortiGate in NAT mode works as L3 device. It means it can route packets based on the information in the routing table. Static and dynamic routing are both supported.

5.1 Static

In static routes there are two main attributes: administrative distance (AD) and priority. In both cases a lower value is preferred. In the routing table only the best path (the best AD) is shown, but you are not limited only to one route with the same destination. Equal cost multipath is supported.

Let's start to analyze a case with two ISPs. You have set AD 10 on route via port1 and AD 15 on route via port2. When you check the routing table it shows only one default route, the one with lower AD:

Example 5.1

```
FG-A # get router info routing-table all


Routing table for VRF=0
Codes: K - kernel, C - connected, S - static, R - RIP, B - BGP
       O - OSPF, IA - OSPF inter area
       N1 - OSPF NSSA external type 1, N2 - OSPF NSSA external type 2
       E1 - OSPF external type 1, E2 - OSPF external type 2
       i - IS-IS, L1 - IS-IS level-1, L2 - IS-IS level-2, ia - IS-IS inter area
       * - candidate default

S*        0.0.0.0/0 [10/0] via 172.16.1.254, port1 <- AD 10 is lowest and active (*)
C         10.0.1.0/24 is directly connected, port3
C         172.16.1.0/24 is directly connected, port1
```

```
C        172.16.2.0/24 is directly connected, port2



FG-A #
```

When you check the routing database, there is one route via port2. You cannot send and receive traffic via port2 if the entry is inactive.

Example 5.2

```
FG-A # get router info routing-table database


Routing table for VRF=0
Codes: K - kernel, C - connected, S - static, R - RIP, B - BGP
       O - OSPF, IA - OSPF inter area
       N1 - OSPF NSSA external type 1, N2 - OSPF NSSA external type 2
       E1 - OSPF external type 1, E2 - OSPF external type 2
       i - IS-IS, L1 - IS-IS level-1, L2 - IS-IS level-2, ia - IS-IS inter area
       > - selected route, * - FIB route, p - stale info


S        0.0.0.0/0 [15/0] via 172.16.2.254, port2, [5/0]  <-entry is not active because AD=15
S     *> 0.0.0.0/0 [10/0] via 172.16.1.254, port1 <- only this route is active
C     *> 10.0.1.0/24 is directly connected, port3
C     *> 172.16.1.0/24 is directly connected, port1
C     *> 172.16.2.0/24 is directly connected, port2


FG-A #
```

In case you expect traffic via the secondary ISP, you can set the same AD but with higher priority (5). Lower priority is preferred, so the FortiGate still prefers forwarding traffic via port1 (in our example):

Example 5.3

```
FG-A # get router info routing-table all


Routing table for VRF=0
Codes: K - kernel, C - connected, S - static, R - RIP, B - BGP
       O - OSPF, IA - OSPF inter area
       N1 - OSPF NSSA external type 1, N2 - OSPF NSSA external type 2
       E1 - OSPF external type 1, E2 - OSPF external type 2
       i - IS-IS, L1 - IS-IS level-1, L2 - IS-IS level-2, ia - IS-IS inter area
       * - candidate default


S*      0.0.0.0/0 [10/0] via 172.16.1.254, port1
                  [10/0] via 172.16.2.254, port2, [5/0]   <- set higher priority
C       10.0.1.0/24 is directly connected, port3
C       172.16.1.0/24 is directly connected, port1
C       172.16.2.0/24 is directly connected, port2



FG-A #
```

In the routing database you see "*****" for both routes. It means both are active:

Example 5.4

```
FG-A # get router info routing-table database


Routing table for VRF=0
Codes: K - kernel, C - connected, S - static, R - RIP, B - BGP
       O - OSPF, IA - OSPF inter area
       N1 - OSPF NSSA external type 1, N2 - OSPF NSSA external type 2
       E1 - OSPF external type 1, E2 - OSPF external type 2
       i - IS-IS, L1 - IS-IS level-1, L2 - IS-IS level-2, ia - IS-IS inter area
       > - selected route, * - FIB route, p - stale info


S    *> 0.0.0.0/0 [10/0] via 172.16.1.254, port1
     *>            [10/0] via 172.16.2.254, port2, [5/0]
C    *> 10.0.1.0/24 is directly connected, port3
C    *> 172.16.1.0/24 is directly connected, port1
C    *> 172.16.2.0/24 is directly connected, port2


FG-A #
```

When the FortiGate receives packets and the traffic is permitted, the route lookup is performed (twice). First time when the session is initiated:

Example 5.5

```
id=20085 trace_id=217 func=print_pkt_detail line=5375 msg="vd-test received a packet(proto=6, 10.16.2.16:22167->172.16.4.10:80) from vlan5. flag [S], seq 4283788036, ack 0, win 4380"

id=20085 trace_id=217 func=init_ip_session_common line=5534 msg="allocate a new session-0c22ee5d"

id=20085 trace_id=217 func=vf_ip_route_input_common line=2574 msg="find a route: flag=00000000 gw-192.168.6.9 via vlan3"
```

```
id=20085 trace_id=217 func=fw_forward_handler line=743 msg="Allowed by Policy-16:"
```

Second time, for the returning traffic:

Example 5.6

```
id=20085 trace_id=218 func=print_pkt_detail line=5375 msg="vd-test received a
packet(proto=6, 172.16.4.10:80->10.16.2.16:22167) from vlan3. flag [S.], seq 3882227979, ack
4283788037, win 28960"

id=20085 trace_id=218 func=resolve_ip_tuple_fast line=5450 msg="Find an existing session,
id-0c22ee5d, reply direction"

id=20085 trace_id=218 func=vf_ip_route_input_common line=2574 msg="find a route:
flag=00000000 gw-192.168.4.3 via vlan5"

id=20085 trace_id=218 func=npu_handle_session44 line=1096 msg="Trying to offloading session
from vlan3 to vlan5, skb.npu_flag=00000400 ses.state=04010204 ses.npu_state=0x00000000"

id=20085 trace_id=218 func=ip_session_install_npu_session line=351 msg="npu session
installation succeeded"
```

Once the session is set up, the routing is no more checked. The only exception is a case you modify the relevant route.

5.1.1 Policy Base Routing

If you need to change standard routing behavior (routing traffic based only on the destination IP), there is Policy Base Routing (PBR). In the below example, for the TCP traffic, from source 10.0.1.10/32 and incoming interface port3 (iif=5) and destination 8.8.8.8/32, the traffic will be sent via port2 (oif=4). On some physical appliances there are two management interfaces (mgmt1 and mgmt2), and that is why port1 index is 3, port2 is 4, and so on (unfortunately I couldn't find any official documentation confirming it).

Example 5.7

```
FG-A # diagnose firewall proute list

list route policy info(vf=root):


id=1 dscp_tag=0xff 0xff flags=0x0 tos=0x00 tos_mask=0x00 protocol=6 sport=0:65535 iif=5
dport=0-65535 oif=4 gwy=8.8.8.8

source(1): 10.0.1.10-10.0.1.10

destination wildcard(1): 8.8.8.8/255.255.255.255


FG-A #
```

You can verify if the PBR works by checking the **diagnose debug flow** output. Here you can find information about a matching policy routing.

Example 5.8

```
id=20085 trace_id=31 func=print_pkt_detail line=5517 msg="vd-root:0 received a
packet(proto=6, 10.0.1.10:50731->10.0.2.10:80) from port3. flag [S], seq 2551198907, ack 0,
win 8192"

id=20085 trace_id=31 func=init_ip_session_common line=5682 msg="allocate a new session-
000022b0"

id=20085 trace_id=31 func=iprope_dnat_check line=4942 msg="in-[port3], out-[]"

id=20085 trace_id=31 func=iprope_dnat_check line=4955 msg="result: skb_flags-02000000, vid-
0, ret-no-match, act-accept, flag-00000000"

id=20085 trace_id=31 func=vf_ip_route_input_common line=2578 msg="Match policy routing: to
10.0.2.10 via ifindex-20" <- PBR

id=20085 trace_id=31 func=vf_ip_route_input_common line=2591 msg="find a route:
flag=04000000 gw-10.0.2.10 via port7"

id=20085 trace_id=31 func=iprope_fwd_check line=726 msg="in-[port3], out-[port7], skb_flags-
02000000, vid-0, app_id: 0, url_cat_id: 0"
```

5.1.2 Link Health Monitor

The Link Health Monitor is a mechanism which monitors the access to a server via a specific interface. When FortiGate is not able to reach the server, it removes the static routes for that exit interface (if the option 'update route' is enabled).

Example 5.9

```
FG-A # diagnose sys link-monitor status


Link Monitor: link2, Status: alive, Server num(1), Create time: Fri Apr  3 00:44:09 2020
Source interface: port2 (4)
Interval: 1
  Peer: 8.8.8.8(8.8.8.8)
        Source IP(172.16.2.1)
        Route: 172.16.2.1->8.8.8.8/32, gwy(172.16.2.254)
        protocol: ping, state: alive
                Latency(Min/Max/Avg): 7.242/16.597/8.326 ms
                Jitter(Min/Max/Avg): 0.033/8.973/0.944
                Packet lost: 0.000%
                Number of out-of-sequence packets: 0
                Fail Times(0/5)
                Packet sent: 34, received: 34, Sequence(sent/rcvd/exp): 35/35/36

FG-A #
```

On the port where the health monitor is enabled, you can check bandwidth, latency, jitter and packet loss:

Example 5.10

```
FG-A # diagnose sys link-monitor interface port2
Interface(port2): state(up, since Fri Apr  3 00:44:09 2020
), bandwidth(up:494bps, down:667bps), session count(0), tx(12874 bytes), rx(678682 bytes), latency(8.48), jitter(0.93), packet-loss(0.00).


FG-A #
```

You can see the probes statistics by **diagnose debug application link-monitor**:

Example 5.11

```
FG-A # diagnose debug enable


FG-A # diagnose debug application link-monitor -1
Debug messages will be on for 30 minutes.


FG-A # lnkmtd::ping_send_msg(275): --> ping 8.8.8.8 seq_no=144, icmp id=0.0, send 40 bytes

lnkmtd; link2(8.8.8.8:ping) send probe packet, fail count(0)

lnkmtd::ping_do_addr_up(61): link2->8.8.8.8(8.8.8.8), rcvd

monitor_peer_recv-1540: lnkmtd:   link2 send time 1585899993s 540233us, revd time 1585899993s 548635us
```

5.2   OSPF

OSPF is one of the most popular dynamic routing protocols among interior gateway protocols (IGP). The network design can be complex as OSPF offers more features than static routing. The intention of this book is not to explain how OSPF works. I assume you already know it.

Let's analyze the below network map (Figure 5.1). There are four FortiGate devices running OSPF. There is one area (backbone) and two ISPs.

Figure 5.1

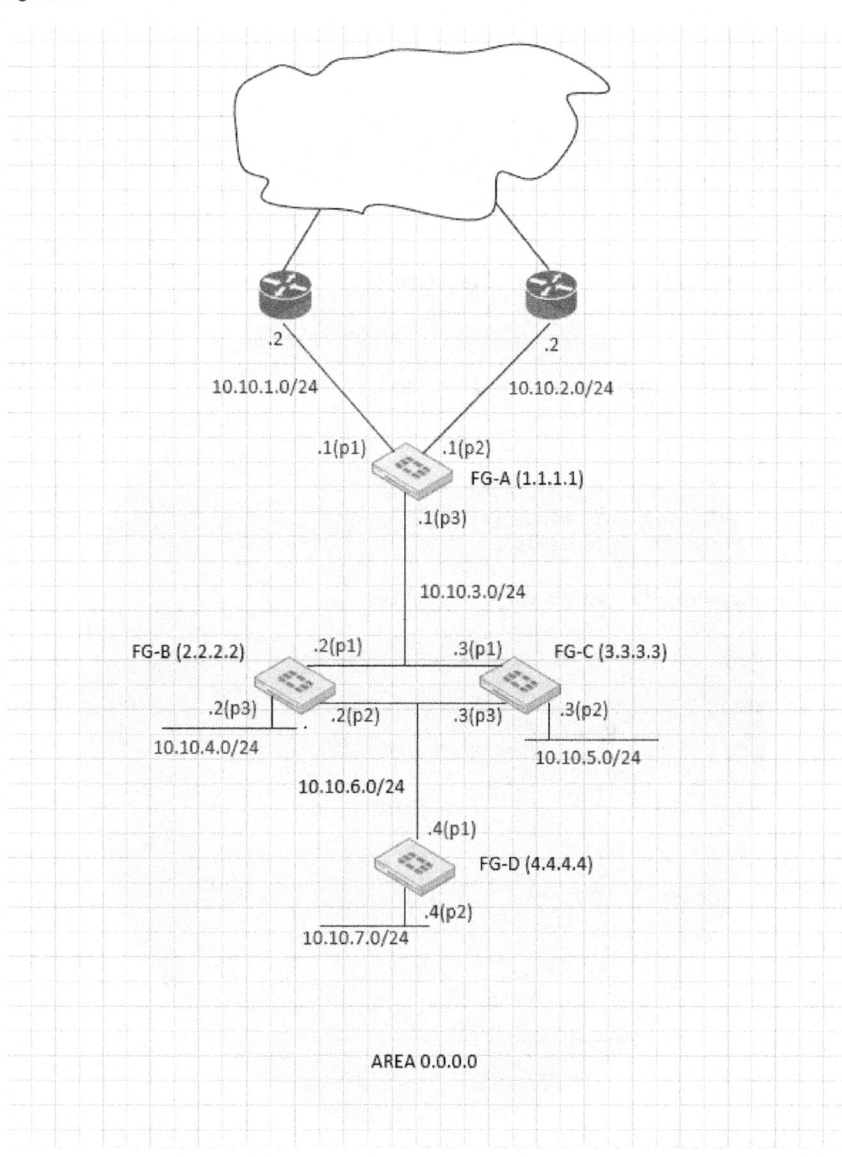

When we do not know what routing protocols are currently in use, we can start by checking information about all protocols:

Example 5.12

```
FG-A # get router info protocols
Routing Protocol is "rip"
  Sending updates every 30 seconds with +/-50%
  Timeout after 180 seconds, garbage collect after 120 seconds
  Outgoing update filter list for all interface is not set
  Incoming update filter list for all interface is not set
  Default redistribution metric is 1
  Maximum output metric is 15
  Redistributing:
  Default version control: send version 2, receive version 2
    Interface        Send  Recv   Key-chain
  Routing for Networks:
  Routing Information Sources:
    Gateway          Distance  Last Update  Bad Packets  Bad Routes
  Distance: (default is 120)

Routing Protocol is "ospf 0"
  Invalid after 0 seconds, hold down 0, flushed after 0
  Outgoing update filter list for all interfaces is
  Incoming update filter list for all interfaces is
  Redistributing:
  Routing for Networks: <- networks for which OSPF is enabled
    10.10.1.0/24
    10.10.2.0/24
    10.10.3.0/24
  Routing Information Sources:
    Gateway          Distance       Last Update
  Distance: (default is 110)
    Address          Mask           Distance List

Routing Protocol is "isis"
System ID: 0000.0000.0000
Area addr: Non-configured
IS type: level-1-2
Number of Neighbors: 0

FG-A #
```

Now you know that OSPF is running. Let's check its status:

Example 5.13

```
FG-A # get router info ospf status
 Routing Process "ospf 0" with ID 1.1.1.1
 Process uptime is 23 minutes
 Process bound to VRF default
 Conforms to RFC2328, and RFC1583Compatibility flag is disabled
 Supports only single TOS(TOS0) routes
 Supports opaque LSA
 Do not support Restarting
 SPF schedule delay 5 secs, Hold time between two SPFs 10 secs
 Refresh timer 10 secs
 Number of incomming current DD exchange neighbors 0/5
 Number of outgoing current DD exchange neighbors 0/5
 Number of external LSA 0. Checksum 0x000000
 Number of opaque AS LSA 0. Checksum 0x000000
 Number of non-default external LSA 0
 External LSA database is unlimited.
 Number of LSA originated 2
 Number of LSA received 16
 Number of areas attached to this router: 1
    Area 0.0.0.0 (BACKBONE) <- there is one area
        Number of interfaces in this area is 3(3)
        Number of fully adjacent neighbors in this area is 2
        Area has no authentication
        SPF algorithm last executed 00:03:08.740 ago
        SPF algorithm executed 7 times
        Number of LSA 6. Checksum 0x035a8c
```

As you can see there are plenty of details about OSPF. You can see the router ID, the confirmation which LSAs are exchanged, what is the area ID and the type of the area. You can also find information about interfaces per area, number of neighbors and if authentication is enabled.

From the above output we know there are two fully adjacent neighbors. The below command shows more details about them:

Example 5.14

```
FG-A # get router info ospf neighbor all

OSPF process 0:
Neighbor ID     Pri   State           Dead Time   Address      Interface
2.2.2.2         1     Full/Backup     00:00:35    10.10.3.2    port3
3.3.3.3         1     Full/DROther    00:00:39    10.10.3.3    port3
```

What we can learn from the above output? First, it must be a broadcast network as you can see BDR (2.2.2.2). This device must be DR because you can see fully adjacency with DROther. Only DR and BDR perform such adjacency.

You can learn more about each of them by adding the **detail** parameter to the previous command:

Example 5.15

```
FG-A # get router info ospf neighbor detail all
OSPF process 0:

 Neighbor 2.2.2.2, interface address 10.10.3.2
    In the area 0.0.0.0 via interface port3
    Neighbor priority is 1, State is Full, 5 state changes
    DR is 10.10.3.1, BDR is 10.10.3.2
    Options is 0x42 (*|O|-|-|-|-|E|-)
    Dead timer due in 00:00:36
    Neighbor is up for 00:20:49
    Database Summary List 0
    Link State Request List 0
    Link State Retransmission List 0
    Crypt Sequence Number is 0
    Thread Inactivity Timer on
    Thread Database Description Retransmission off
    Thread Link State Request Retransmission off
    Thread Link State Update Retransmission off

 Neighbor 3.3.3.3, interface address 10.10.3.3
    In the area 0.0.0.0 via interface port3
    Neighbor priority is 1, State is Full, 4 state changes
    DR is 10.10.3.1, BDR is 10.10.3.2
    Options is 0x42 (*|O|-|-|-|-|E|-)
    Dead timer due in 00:00:40
    Neighbor is up for 00:19:56
    Database Summary List 0
    Link State Request List 0
    Link State Retransmission List 0
    Crypt Sequence Number is 0
    Thread Inactivity Timer on
    Thread Database Description Retransmission off
    Thread Link State Request Retransmission off
    Thread Link State Update Retransmission off
```

OSPF exchanges LSA information by sending LSU packets, and every router builds its own map of the network. The information is stored in their local database:

Example 5.16

```
FG-A # get router info ospf database brief

            Router Link States (Area 0.0.0.0)

Link ID         ADV Router      Age   Seq#      CkSum Flag Link count
1.1.1.1         1.1.1.1         1195  80000005  5a6f  0031 3
2.2.2.2         2.2.2.2         234   80000008  8415  0012 3
3.3.3.3         3.3.3.3         235   80000006  850b  0012 3
4.4.4.4         4.4.4.4         209   80000006  893e  0012 2

            Net Link States (Area 0.0.0.0)

Link ID         ADV Router      Age   Seq#      CkSum Flag
10.10.3.1       1.1.1.1         1195  80000002  9090  0021
10.10.6.2       2.2.2.2         234   80000002  dd2f  0002


FG-A #
```

You can see more details about each LSA type in the database with the below command:

Example 5.17

```
FG-A # get router info ospf database router lsa

            Router Link States (Area 0.0.0.0)

  LS age: 1203
  Options: 0x2 (*|-|-|-|-|-|E|-)
  Flags: 0x0
  LS Type: router-LSA
  Link State ID: 1.1.1.1
  Advertising Router: 1.1.1.1
  LS Seq Number: 80000005
  Checksum: 0x5a6f
  Length: 60
  Number of Links: 3

    Link connected to: Stub Network
      (Link ID) Network/subnet number: 10.10.1.0
      (Link Data) Network Mask: 255.255.255.0
```

```
    Number of TOS metrics: 0
     TOS 0 Metric: 1

  Link connected to: Stub Network
   (Link ID) Network/subnet number: 10.10.2.0
   (Link Data) Network Mask: 255.255.255.0
    Number of TOS metrics: 0
     TOS 0 Metric: 1

  Link connected to: a Transit Network
   (Link ID) Designated Router address: 10.10.3.1
   (Link Data) Router Interface address: 10.10.3.1
    Number of TOS metrics: 0
     TOS 0 Metric: 1
```

The next command provides more details about the interface settings. Before the router can establish OSPF neighborship, it needs to agree on the following settings:

- IP address and mask (point-to-point may ignore the mask length)
- The same area ID
- The same MTU
- The same network types
- Time intervals
- Authentication

Example 5.18

```
FG-A # get router info ospf interface
port1 is up, line protocol is up
  Internet Address 10.10.1.1/24, Area 0.0.0.0, MTU 1500
  Process ID 0, Router ID 1.1.1.1, Network Type BROADCAST, Cost: 1
  Transmit Delay is 1 sec, State DR, Priority 1
  Designated Router (ID) 1.1.1.1, Interface Address 10.10.1.1
  No backup designated router on this network
  Timer intervals configured, Hello 10.000, Dead 40, Wait 40, Retransmit 5
    Hello due in 00:00:00
  Neighbor Count is 0, Adjacent neighbor count is 0
  Crypt Sequence Number is 10
  Hello received 0 sent 149, DD received 0 sent 0
  LS-Req received 0 sent 0, LS-Upd received 0 sent 0
  LS-Ack received 0 sent 0, Discarded 0
```

Let's see what is in the routing table:

Example 5.19

```
FG-A # get router info ospf route
C   10.10.1.0/24 [1] is directly connected, port1, Area 0.0.0.0
C   10.10.2.0/24 [1] is directly connected, port2, Area 0.0.0.0
C   10.10.3.0/24 [1] is directly connected, port3, Area 0.0.0.0
O   10.10.4.0/24 [2] via 10.10.3.2, port3, Area 0.0.0.0
O   10.10.5.0/24 [2] via 10.10.3.3, port3, Area 0.0.0.0
O   10.10.6.0/24 [2] via 10.10.3.2, port3, Area 0.0.0.0
                      via 10.10.3.3, port3, Area 0.0.0.0
O   10.10.7.0/24 [3] via 10.10.3.2, port3, Area 0.0.0.0
                      via 10.10.3.3, port3, Area 0.0.0.0

FG-A #
```

The above scenario is not complex because there is only one area, no summarization, etc.

Let's analyze the below network diagram, where you can see a more complex design. There are five areas, including NSSA and stub area.

Figure 5.2

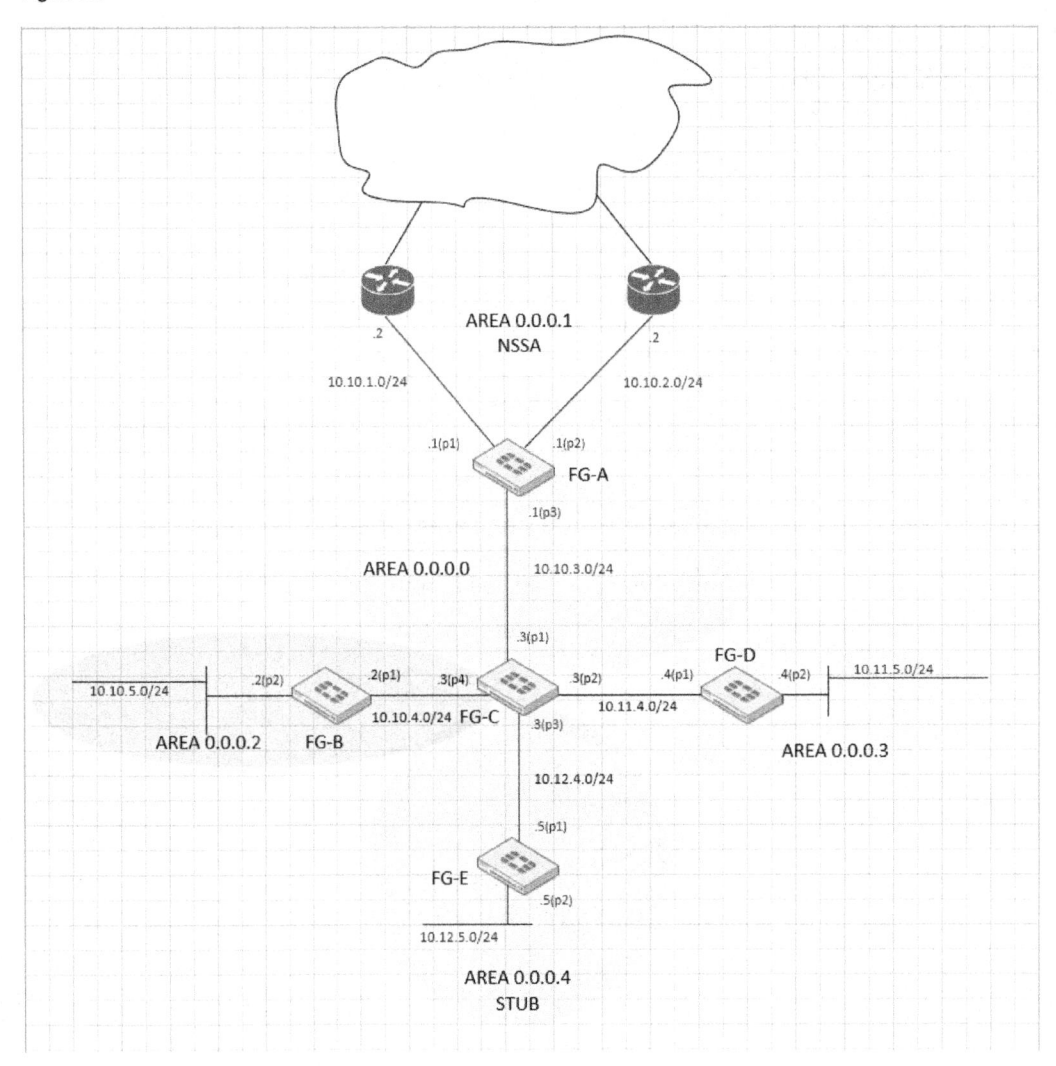

and the routing table on FG-E, which is in the stub area:

Example 5.20

```
FG-E # get router info routing-table all
Codes: K - kernel, C - connected, S - static, R - RIP, B - BGP
       O - OSPF, IA - OSPF inter area
```

```
            N1 - OSPF NSSA external type 1, N2 - OSPF NSSA external type 2
            E1 - OSPF external type 1, E2 - OSPF external type 2
            i - IS-IS, L1 - IS-IS level-1, L2 - IS-IS level-2, ia - IS-IS inter area
            * - candidate default

O*IA     0.0.0.0/0 [110/11] via 10.12.4.3, port1, 00:02:28   <- default gateway (because of
stub area)
O IA     10.10.1.0/24 [110/3] via 10.12.4.3, port1, 00:02:28
O IA     10.10.2.0/24 [110/3] via 10.12.4.3, port1, 00:02:28
O IA     10.10.3.0/24 [110/2] via 10.12.4.3, port1, 00:02:28
O IA     10.10.4.0/24 [110/2] via 10.12.4.3, port1, 00:02:28
O IA     10.10.5.0/24 [110/3] via 10.12.4.3, port1, 00:02:28
C        10.10.10.0/24 is directly connected, port10
O IA     10.11.4.0/24 [110/2] via 10.12.4.3, port1, 00:02:28
O IA     10.11.5.0/24 [110/3] via 10.12.4.3, port1, 00:02:28
C        10.12.4.0/24 is directly connected, port1
C        10.12.5.0/24 is directly connected, port2

FG-E #
```

OSPF area on FG-E is the stub and that's why you can see the default gateway. Depending on the firmware version, you can find individual routes or just only the summary/default one. You can remove all non-summary prefixes by setting **set stub-type no-summary**:

Example 5.21

```
FG-E (0.0.0.4) # show
config area
    edit 0.0.0.4
        set type stub
    next
end

FG-E (0.0.0.4) # show full-configuration
config area
    edit 0.0.0.4
        set shortcut disable
        set authentication none
        set default-cost 10
        set stub-type no-summary  <- it removes all non-summary prefixes
        set type stub
    next
end

FG-E
```

Once you change the configuration, you should see only the summary route:

Example 5.22

```
FG-E # get router info routing-table all
Codes: K - kernel, C - connected, S - static, R - RIP, B - BGP
       O - OSPF, IA - OSPF inter area
       N1 - OSPF NSSA external type 1, N2 - OSPF NSSA external type 2
       E1 - OSPF external type 1, E2 - OSPF external type 2
       i - IS-IS, L1 - IS-IS level-1, L2 - IS-IS level-2, ia - IS-IS inter area
       * - candidate default

O*IA   0.0.0.0/0 [110/11] via 10.12.4.3, port1, 00:00:04
C      10.10.10.0/24 is directly connected, port10
C      10.12.4.0/24 is directly connected, port1
C      10.12.5.0/24 is directly connected, port2

FG-E #
```

In case you see a problem with OSPF neighborship like the one below:

Example 5.23

```
FG-A # get router info ospf neighbor

OSPF process 0:
Neighbor ID     Pri   State            Dead Time   Address      Interface
3.3.3.3          1    ExStart/Backup   00:00:38    10.10.3.3    port3


FG-A #
```

Make sure all the requirements (IP, subnet, area type and ID, MTU, authentication) are met. The below diagnose commands help to find out what the issue is:

Example 5.24

```
diagnose ip router ospf all enable
diagnose ip router ospf level info
```

```
diagnose debug enable


diagnose sniffer packet any "proto 89" 4
```

The problem with authentication is quite easy to spot. You can see the error "authentication type mismatch" in the message from FG-C (router ID 3.3.3.3).

Example 5.25

```
OSPF: RECV[Hello]: From 3.3.3.3 via port3:10.10.3.1 (10.10.3.3 -> 224.0.0.5)
OSPF: -----------------------------------------------------
OSPF: Header
OSPF:    Version 2
OSPF:    Type 1 (Hello)
OSPF:    Packet Len 44
OSPF:    Router ID 3.3.3.3
OSPF:    Area ID 0.0.0.0
OSPF:    Checksum 0xe98b
OSPF:    AuType 0 <- no authentication
OSPF: Hello
OSPF:    NetworkMask 255.255.255.0
OSPF:    HelloInterval 10
OSPF:    Options 0x2 (*|-|-|-|-|-|E|-)
OSPF:    RtrPriority 1
OSPF:    RtrDeadInterval 40
OSPF:    DRouter 10.10.3.3
OSPF:    BDRouter 0.0.0.0
OSPF:    # Neighbors 0
OSPF: -----------------------------------------------------
OSPF: RECV[Hello]: From 3.3.3.3 via port3:10.10.3.1: Authentication type mismatch
```

On the other router there is no the same message, but you can see what authentication type in the hello message is: "2" MD5 authentication.

Example 5.26

```
OSPF: SEND[Hello]: To 224.0.0.5 via port3:10.10.3.1, length 60
OSPF: ----------------------------------------------------
OSPF: Header
OSPF:     Version 2
OSPF:     Type 1 (Hello)
OSPF:     Packet Len 44
OSPF:     Router ID 1.1.1.1
OSPF:     Area ID 0.0.0.0
OSPF:     Checksum 0x0
OSPF:     AuType 2 <- MD5 authentication
OSPF:     Cryptographic Authentication
OSPF:     Key ID 0
OSPF:     Auth Data Len 16
OSPF:     Sequence number 18
OSPF: Hello
OSPF:     NetworkMask 255.255.255.0
OSPF:     HelloInterval 10
OSPF:     Options 0x2 (*|-|-|-|-|-|E|-)
OSPF:     RtrPriority 1
OSPF:     RtrDeadInterval 40
OSPF:     DRouter 10.10.3.1
OSPF:     BDRouter 0.0.0.0
OSPF:     # Neighbors 0
OSPF: ----------------------------------------------------
```

The "ExStart" state, can be caused by mismatch MTU. The problem is, you do not see the clear error message. There is only message "negotiation fails". However, the MTU size is shown in the debug output, and in the OSPF interface settings.

Example 5.27

```
OSPF: RECV[DD]: From 1.1.1.1 via port1:10.10.3.3 (10.10.3.1 -> 10.10.3.3)
OSPF: ----------------------------------------------------
OSPF: Header
OSPF:     Version 2
OSPF:     Type 2 (Database Description)
OSPF:     Packet Len 32
OSPF:     Router ID 1.1.1.1
OSPF:     Area ID 0.0.0.0
OSPF:     Checksum 0xb327
OSPF:     AuType 0
OSPF: Database Description
OSPF:     Interface MTU 1494 <- MTU size
OSPF:     Options 0x42 (*|O|-|-|-|-|E|-)
OSPF:     Bits 7 (-|I|M|MS)
OSPF:     Sequence Number 0x000000d7
OSPF:     # LSA Headers 0
OSPF: ----------------------------------------------------
OSPF: RECV[DD]: From 1.1.1.1 via port1:10.10.3.3: Negotiation fails, packet discarded
OSPF: NFSM[port1:10.10.3.3-1.1.1.1]: DD Retransmit timer expire
```

And in the send hello packet:

Example 5.28

```
OSPF: SEND[DD]: To 10.10.3.1 via port1:10.10.3.3, length 32
OSPF: -------------------------------------------------
OSPF: Header
OSPF:    Version 2
OSPF:    Type 2 (Database Description)
OSPF:    Packet Len 32
OSPF:    Router ID 3.3.3.3
OSPF:    Area ID 0.0.0.0
OSPF:    Checksum 0xafe4
OSPF:    AuType 0
OSPF: Database Description
OSPF:    Interface MTU 1500 <- MTU size
OSPF:    Options 0x42 (*|O|-|-|-|E|-)
OSPF:    Bits 7 (-|I|M|MS)
OSPF:    Sequence Number 0x00000010
OSPF:    # LSA Headers 0
OSPF: -------------------------------------------------
```

You need to compare the output from the two devices to see if there is any difference. FG-C on port1 has MTU 1500:

Example 5.29

```
FG-C # get router info ospf interface port1
port1 is up, line protocol is up
  Internet Address 10.10.3.3/24, Area 0.0.0.0, MTU 1500
  Process ID 0, VRF 0, Router ID 3.3.3.3, Network Type BROADCAST, Cost: 1
  Transmit Delay is 1 sec, State Backup, Priority 1
```

```
  Designated Router (ID) 1.1.1.1, Interface Address 10.10.3.1
  Backup Designated Router (ID) 3.3.3.3, Interface Address 10.10.3.3
  Timer intervals configured, Hello 10.000, Dead 40, Wait 40, Retransmit 5
    Hello due in 00:00:07
  Neighbor Count is 1, Adjacent neighbor count is 0
  Crypt Sequence Number is 9
  Hello received 58 sent 59, DD received 116 sent 116
  LS-Req received 0 sent 0, LS-Upd received 0 sent 0
  LS-Ack received 0 sent 0, Discarded 0


FG-C #
```

And FG-A on port3 has MTU 1494. There should be the same value on both interfaces. Otherwise they cannot establish the neighborship.

Example 5.30

```
FG-A # get router info ospf interface port3
port3 is up, line protocol is up
  Internet Address 10.10.3.1/24, Area 0.0.0.0, MTU 1494
  Process ID 0, VRF 0, Router ID 1.1.1.1, Network Type BROADCAST, Cost: 1
  Transmit Delay is 1 sec, State DR, Priority 1
  Designated Router (ID) 1.1.1.1, Interface Address 10.10.3.1
  Backup Designated Router (ID) 3.3.3.3, Interface Address 10.10.3.3
  Timer intervals configured, Hello 10.000, Dead 40, Wait 40, Retransmit 5
    Hello due in 00:00:03
  Neighbor Count is 1, Adjacent neighbor count is 0
  Crypt Sequence Number is 10
  Hello received 67 sent 86, DD received 0 sent 132
```

```
LS-Req received 0 sent 0, LS-Upd received 0 sent 0

LS-Ack received 0 sent 0, Discarded 132
```

5.3 BGP

The only one Exterior Gateway Protocol used in the Internet is BGP and it is supported by FortiGate. As you may already know, it can be implemented in two different variations: internal BGP (iBGP) or external (eBGP). Here I present the most popular use case: two ISPs and traffic engineering.

The goal here is to forward traffic to 197.1.1.0/24 and 198.1.1.0/24 via port1, connected to the ISP1.

Figure 5.3

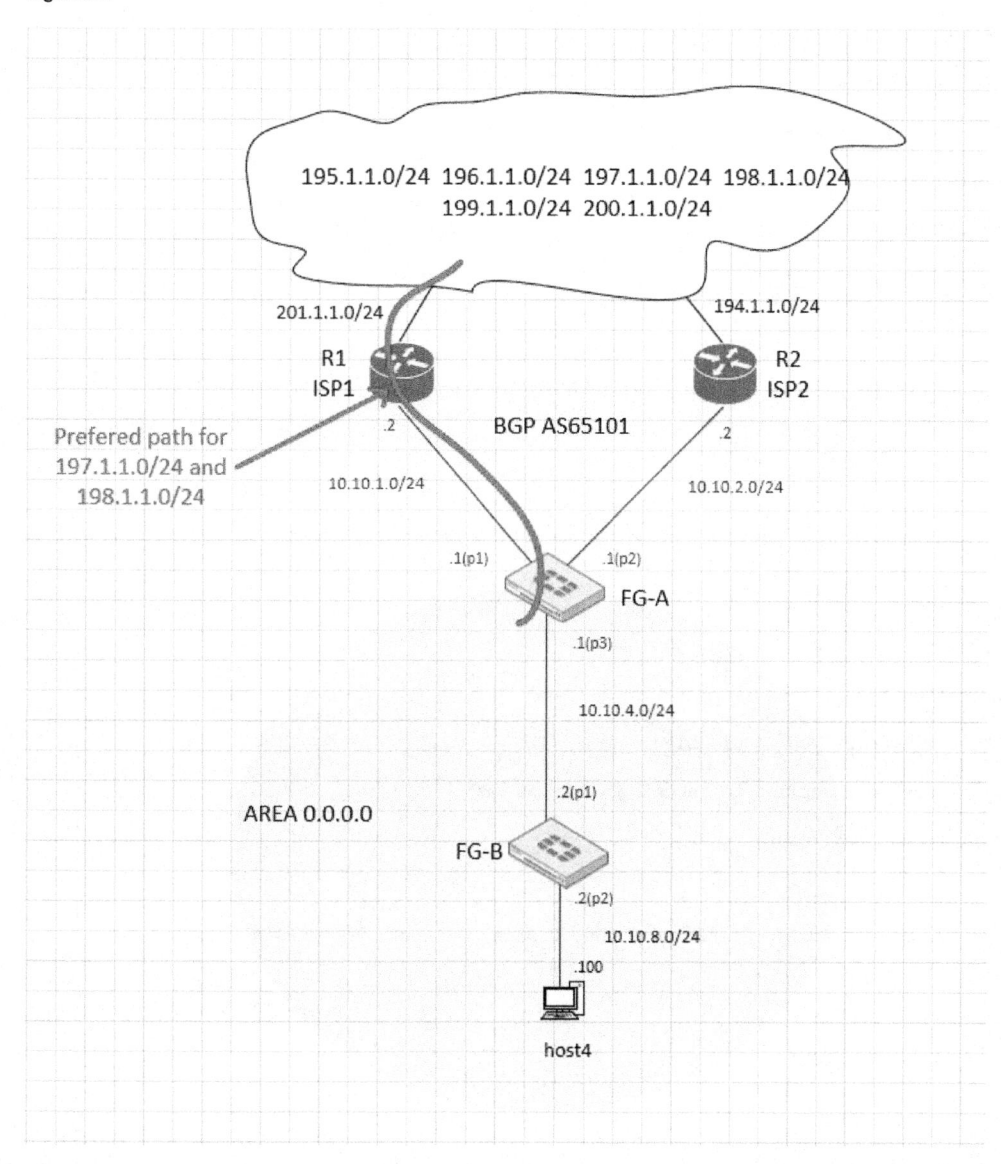

195.1.1.0/24 196.1.1.0/24 197.1.1.0/24 198.1.1.0/24
199.1.1.0/24 200.1.1.0/24

201.1.1.0/24   194.1.1.0/24

R1   R2
ISP1   ISP2

Prefered path for
197.1.1.0/24 and   BGP AS65101
198.1.1.0/24
                    10.10.1.0/24   10.10.2.0/24

                        .1(p1)   .1(p2)
                                FG-A
                            .1(p3)

                        10.10.4.0/24

                            .2(p1)
AREA 0.0.0.0
                            FG-B
                            .2(p2)
                                    10.10.8.0/24
                            .100

                            host4

Let's analyze the current BGP configuration by using the below commands:

Example 5.31

```
get router info protocols
get router info bgp summary
get router info bgp network
get router info routing-table bgp
diagnose ip router bgp level info
diagnose ip router bgp all enable
diagnose debug enable
```

As you can see, the route map is applied on the neighbor 10.10.1.2, which is ISP1 (R1):

Example 5.32

```
FG-A # get router info protocols
...
Routing Protocol is "bgp 65101"
  IGP synchronization is disabled
  Automatic route summarization is disabled
  Default local-preference applied to incoming route is 100
  Redistributing: connected, ospf
  Neighbor(s):
    Address         AddressFamily  FiltIn  FiltOut  DistIn  DistOut  RouteMapIn          RouteMapOut
    Weight
    10.10.1.2                      unicast                                    pref-197-198-isp1root
    10.10.2.2                      unicast

FG-A #
```

The status of both neighbors is up and all messages between FG-A and its BGP neighbors are correctly exchanged.

Example 5.33

```
FG-A # get router info bgp summary
BGP router identifier 1.1.1.1, local AS number 65101
BGP table version is 4
1 BGP AS-PATH entries
0 BGP community entries


Neighbor           V        AS MsgRcvd MsgSent    TblVer  InQ OutQ Up/Down  State/PfxRcd
10.10.1.2          4     65101      10      10         3    0    0 00:06:06            2
10.10.2.2          4     65101      12      12         2    0    0 00:07:56            8


Total number of neighbors 2


FG-A #
```

The command **get router info bgp network** shows that the path for most of the prefixes is via ISP2. As specified above, only two prefixes should be reachable via ISP1 (next hop 10.10.1.2).

Example 5.34

```
FG-A # get router info bgp network
BGP table version is 4, local router ID is 1.1.1.1
Status codes: s suppressed, d damped, h history, * valid, > best, i - internal,
              S Stale
Origin codes: i - IGP, e - EGP, ? - incomplete


   Network           Next Hop            Metric LocPrf Weight RouteTag Path
```

```
*> 10.10.1.0/24      0.0.0.0                    32768     0 ?
*                    0.0.0.0             100    32768     0 i
*  i10.10.2.0/24     10.10.2.2     0     100    0         0 I
*>                   0.0.0.0                    32768     0 ?
*                    0.0.0.0             100    32768     0 i
*> 10.10.4.0/24      0.0.0.0                    32768     0 ?
*> 10.10.8.0/24      10.10.4.2     2            32768     0 ? <- path to area 0.0.0.0
*> 10.10.10.0/24     0.0.0.0                    32768     0 ?
*>i194.1.1.0         10.10.2.2     0     100    0         0 i
*>i195.1.1.0         10.10.2.2     0     100    0         0 i
*>i196.1.1.0         10.10.2.2     0     100    0         0 i
*>i197.1.1.0         10.10.1.2     0     200    0         0 i <- via ISP1
*  i                 10.10.2.2     0     100    0         0 i
*>i198.1.1.0         10.10.1.2     0     200    0         0 i <- via ISP1
*  i                 10.10.2.2     0     100    0         0 i
*>i199.1.1.0         10.10.2.2     0     100    0         0 i
*>i200.1.1.0         10.10.2.2     0     100    0         0 i


Total number of prefixes 12


FG-A #
```

In the routing table we can see summary of the details from the above table:

Example 5.35

```
FG-A # get router info routing-table bgp

Routing table for VRF=0
```

```
B        194.1.1.0/24 [200/0] via 10.10.2.2, port2, 00:08:40
B        195.1.1.0/24 [200/0] via 10.10.2.2, port2, 00:08:40
B        196.1.1.0/24 [200/0] via 10.10.2.2, port2, 00:08:40
B        197.1.1.0/24 [200/0] via 10.10.1.2, port1, 00:06:50 <- via ISP1
B        198.1.1.0/24 [200/0] via 10.10.1.2, port1, 00:06:50 <- via ISP1
B        199.1.1.0/24 [200/0] via 10.10.2.2, port2, 00:08:40
B        200.1.1.0/24 [200/0] via 10.10.2.2, port2, 00:08:40


FG-A #
```

When you want to monitor the initial packets exchange, you can reset the BGP neighborship:

Example 5.36

```
execute router clear bgp all
```

And enable the debug commands:

Example 5.37

```
diagnose ip router bgp level info
diagnose ip router bgp all enable
diagnose debug enable
```

Both neighbors are down because of: "User reset".

Example 5.38

```
id=20300 logdesc="BGP neighbor status changed" msg="BGP: %BGP-5-ADJCHANGE: neighbor
10.10.1.2 Down BGP Notification CEASE"

id=20300 logdesc="BGP neighbor status changed" msg="BGP: %BGP-5-ADJCHANGE: neighbor
10.10.1.2 Down User reset"

id=20300 logdesc="BGP neighbor status changed" msg="BGP: %BGP-5-ADJCHANGE: neighbor
10.10.2.2 Down BGP Notification CEASE"

id=20300 logdesc="BGP neighbor status changed" msg="BGP: %BGP-5-ADJCHANGE: neighbor
10.10.2.2 Down User reset"
```

After exchanging a couple of packets and moving through all BGP states (**Idle -> Connect -> Active -> OpenSent -> OpenConfirm -> Established**), the BGP peering is finally up:

Example 5.39

```
BGP: 10.10.2.2-Outgoing [FSM] State: Idle Event: 3

BGP: 10.10.2.2-Outgoing [NETWORK] FD=21, Sock Status: 113-No route to host

BGP: 10.10.2.2-Outgoing [FSM] State: Connect Event: 18

BGP: 10.10.2.2-Outgoing [FSM] State: Active Event: 14

BGP: 10.10.2.2-Outgoing [FSM] InConnReq: Accepting...

BGP: 10.10.2.2-Outgoing [NETWORK] FD=23, Sock Status: 0-Success

BGP: 10.10.2.2-Outgoing [FSM] State: Active Event: 17

BGP: 10.10.2.2-Outgoing [ENCODE] Msg-Hdr: Type 1

BGP: 10.10.2.2-Outgoing [ENCODE] Open: Ver 4 MyAS 65101 Holdtime 180

BGP: 10.10.2.2-Outgoing [ENCODE] Open: Msg-Size 61

BGP: 10.10.2.2-Outgoing [DECODE] Msg-Hdr: type 1, length 53

BGP: 10.10.2.2-Outgoing [DECODE] Open: Optional param len 24

BGP: 10.10.2.2-Outgoing [DECODE] Open Opt: Option Type 2, Option Len 6

BGP: 10.10.2.2-Outgoing [DECODE] Open Cap: Cap Code 1, Cap Len 4

BGP: 10.10.2.2-Outgoing [DECODE] Open Opt: Option Type 2, Option Len 2

BGP: 10.10.2.2-Outgoing [DECODE] Open Cap: Cap Code 128, Cap Len 0

BGP: 10.10.2.2-Outgoing [DECODE] Open Cap: RR Cap(old) for all address-families
```

```
BGP: 10.10.2.2-Outgoing [DECODE] Open Opt: Option Type 2, Option Len 2
BGP: 10.10.2.2-Outgoing [DECODE] Open Cap: Cap Code 2, Cap Len 0
BGP: 10.10.2.2-Outgoing [DECODE] Open Cap: RR Cap(new) for all address-families
BGP: 10.10.2.2-Outgoing [DECODE] Open Opt: Option Type 2, Option Len 6
BGP: 10.10.2.2-Outgoing [DECODE] Open Cap: Cap Code 65, Cap Len 4
BGP: 10.10.2.2-Outgoing [FSM] State: OpenSent Event: 19
BGP: 10.10.2.2-Outgoing [ENCODE] Msg-Hdr: Type 4
BGP: 10.10.2.2-Outgoing [ENCODE] Keepalive: 15 KAlive msg(s) sent
BGP: 10.10.2.2-Outgoing [DECODE] Msg-Hdr: type 4, length 19
BGP: 10.10.2.2-Outgoing [DECODE] KAlive: Received!
BGP: 10.10.2.2-Outgoing [FSM] State: OpenConfirm Event: 26
BGP: 10.10.2.2-Outgoing [DECODE] Msg-Hdr: type 4, length 19
BGP: 10.10.2.2-Outgoing [DECODE] KAlive: Received!
BGP: 10.10.2.2-Outgoing [FSM] State: Established Event: 26
id=20300 logdesc="BGP neighbor status changed" msg="BGP: %BGP-5-ADJCHANGE: neighbor 10.10.2.2 Up "
```

In the next step, once the neighborship is established, ISP2 sends the update with all its prefixes:

Example 5.40

```
BGP: 10.10.2.2-Outgoing [FSM] State: Established Event: 34
BGP: 10.10.2.2-Outgoing [ENCODE] Msg-Hdr: Type 2
BGP: 10.10.2.2-Outgoing [ENCODE] Attr IP-Unicast: Tot-attr-len 21
BGP: 10.10.2.2-Outgoing [ENCODE] Update: Msg #3 Size 60
BGP: 10.10.2.2-Outgoing [ENCODE] Msg-Hdr: Type 2
BGP: 10.10.2.2-Outgoing [ENCODE] Attr IP-Unicast: Tot-attr-len 28
BGP: 10.10.2.2-Outgoing [ENCODE] Update: Msg #4 Size 55
BGP: 10.10.2.2-Outgoing [DECODE] Msg-Hdr: type 2, length 84
```

```
BGP: 10.10.2.2-Outgoing [DECODE] Update: Starting UPDATE decoding... Bytes To Read (65), msg_size (65)

BGP: 10.10.2.2-Outgoing [DECODE] Update: NLRI Len(32)

BGP: 10.10.2.2-Outgoing [FSM] State: Established Event: 27

BGP: 10.10.2.2-Outgoing [RIB] Update: Received Prefix 10.10.2.0/24

BGP: 10.10.2.2-Outgoing [RIB] Update: Received Prefix 200.1.1.0/24

BGP: 10.10.2.2-Outgoing [RIB] Update: Received Prefix 199.1.1.0/24

BGP: 10.10.2.2-Outgoing [RIB] Update: Received Prefix 198.1.1.0/24

BGP: 10.10.2.2-Outgoing [RIB] Update: Received Prefix 197.1.1.0/24

BGP: 10.10.2.2-Outgoing [RIB] Update: Received Prefix 196.1.1.0/24

BGP: 10.10.2.2-Outgoing [RIB] Update: Received Prefix 195.1.1.0/24

BGP: 10.10.2.2-Outgoing [RIB] Update: Received Prefix 194.1.1.0/24
```

The above scenario does not have any problems. All prefixes are exchanged and all BGP peers are up. What can you do when you see a problem like the one below?

Example 5.41

```
FG-A # get router info bgp summary
BGP router identifier 1.1.1.1, local AS number 65101
BGP table version is 2
1 BGP AS-PATH entries
0 BGP community entries


Neighbor        V      AS  MsgRcvd MsgSent   TblVer  InQ OutQ Up/Down   State/PfxRcd
10.10.1.2       4   65101      27      32        1    0    0 00:00:18             2
10.10.2.2       4   65101      25      29        0    0    0 00:00:26        Active


Total number of neighbors 2
```

The state "Active" means there is a problem with TCP session between the BGP peers. Let's check what the output **diagnose sniffer** command shows:

Example 5.42

```
FG-A # diagnose sniffer packet any 'host 10.10.2.2 and tcp and port 179' 4 a
interfaces=[any]
filters=[host 10.10.2.2 and tcp and port 179]
8.418737 port2 in 10.10.2.2.41850 -> 10.10.2.1.179: syn 246923848
9.418945 port2 in 10.10.2.2.41850 -> 10.10.2.1.179: syn 246923848
11.417101 port2 in 10.10.2.2.41850 -> 10.10.2.1.179: syn 246923848
15.409141 port2 in 10.10.2.2.41850 -> 10.10.2.1.179: syn 246923848
23.395763 port2 in 10.10.2.2.41850 -> 10.10.2.1.179: syn 246923848
```

There are only TCP SYN packets sent by R2(ISP2) and there is no reply sent by FG-A. The command **diagnose debug flow** on FG-A shows more details:

Example 5.43

```
id=20085 trace_id=4 func=print_pkt_detail line=5384 msg="vd-root:0 received a
packet(proto=6, 10.10.2.2:41852->10.10.2.1:179) from port2. flag [S], seq 1708216250, ack 0,
win 29200"

id=20085 trace_id=4 func=init_ip_session_common line=5544 msg="allocate a new session-
00000b80"

id=20085 trace_id=4 func=vf_ip_route_input_common line=2591 msg="find a route: flag=84000000
gw-10.10.2.1 via root"

id=20085 trace_id=4 func=fw_local_in_handler line=409 msg="iprope_in_check() check failed on
policy 1, drop"
```

The reason why FG-A does not send TCP SYN/ACK is a policy #1. The firewall policies, which permit or deny transit traffic, do not control traffic "to" or "from" the firewall. Local-in policy controls it:

Example 5.44

```
FG-A (1) # sh
config firewall local-in-policy
    edit 1
        set intf "port2"
        set srcaddr "all"
        set dstaddr "all"
        set service "BGP"
        set schedule "always"
    next
end
```

Once BGP is allowed by the local-in-policy, the BGP peering moves to up state.

6 High Availability

In case, where high availability is mandatory, FortiGate can work as a HA cluster. You may experience many problems during the initial set up such as failover, or config synchronization. FortiGate supports the proprietary FortiGate Clustering Protocol (FGCP) and Virtual Router Redundancy Protocol (VRRP). They work totally different. FGCP is the primary choice if you have at least two identical devices. They can work in active-passive or active-active mode. VRRP is an RFC standard (RFC 5798) and it does not provide HA cluster member config synchronization. It should be used when you have different FortiGate models or devices.

6.1 FortiGate Clustering Protocol (FGCP)

From the output of the below command you can get a general overview of the HA status:

Example 6.1

```
FG-B # get system status
Version: FortiGate-VM64 v5.6.6,build1630,180913 (GA)
Virus-DB: 1.00123(2015-12-11 13:18)
Extended DB: 1.00000(2012-10-17 15:46)
IPS-DB: 6.00741(2015-12-01 02:30)
IPS-ETDB: 0.00000(2001-01-01 00:00)
APP-DB: 6.00741(2015-12-01 02:30)
INDUSTRIAL-DB: 6.00741(2015-12-01 02:30)
Serial-Number: FGVMEVU7FZZYAIE7
IPS Malicious URL Database: 1.00001(2015-01-01 01:01)
Botnet DB: 1.00000(2012-05-28 22:51)
License Status: Valid
Evaluation License Expires: Sat Nov 17 06:41:47 2018
VM Resources: 1 CPU/1 allowed, 995 MB RAM/1024 MB allowed
BIOS version: 04000002
Log hard disk: Available
Hostname: FG-B
Operation Mode: NAT
Current virtual domain: root
Max number of virtual domains: 1
Virtual domains status: 1 in NAT mode, 0 in TP mode
Virtual domain configuration: disable
FIPS-CC mode: disable
Current HA mode: a-p, master       <- confirmation HA is enabled in active-passive mode, the
```

```
device is master
Cluster uptime: 14 minutes, 6 seconds
Cluster state change time: 2018-11-11 14:21:37
Branch point: 1630
Release Version Information: GA
FortiOS x86-64: Yes
System time: Sun Nov 11 14:22:38 2018

FG-B #
```

You see that HA is enabled, the mode is active-passive (a-p), and FG-B is HA master.

The command **get system ha status** provides more details about HA status:

Example 6.2

```
FG-B # get system ha status
HA Health Status: OK
Model: FortiGate-VM64
Mode: HA A-P
Group: 0
Debug: 0
Cluster Uptime: 0 days 00:14:16
Cluster state change time: 2018-11-11 14:21:37
Master selected using:
    <2018/11/11 14:21:37> FGVMEVU7FZZYAIE7 is selected as the master because it has the
largest value of override priority.
    <2018/11/11 14:21:22> FGVMEVU7FZZYAIE7 is selected as the master because it has the
largest value of uptime.
    <2018/11/11 14:08:48> FGVMEVU7FZZYAIE7 is selected as the master because it's the only
member in the cluster.
ses_pickup: enable, ses_pickup_delay=disable
override: disable
Configuration Status:
    FGVMEVU7FZZYAIE7(updated 5 seconds ago): in-sync
    FGVMEVQGU8XTKE11(updated 5 seconds ago): out-of-sync
    FGVMEVECFB0ZBBDC(updated 3 seconds ago): out-of-sync
System Usage stats:
System Usage stats:
    FGVMEVU7FZZYAIE7(updated 5 seconds ago):
        sessions=2, average-cpu-user/nice/system/idle=0%/0%/0%/100%, memory=61% <-
utilization of members
    FGVMEVQGU8XTKE11(updated 5 seconds ago):
        sessions=0, average-cpu-user/nice/system/idle=0%/0%/0%/100%, memory=60% <-
utilization of members
    FGVMEVECFB0ZBBDC(updated 3 seconds ago):
        sessions=0, average-cpu-user/nice/system/idle=0%/0%/0%/100%, memory=55% <-
utilization of members
```

```
HBDEV stats:   <- heartbeat status
    FGVMEVU7FZZYAIE7(updated 5 seconds ago):
        port9: physical/1000auto, up, rx-bytes/packets/dropped/errors=454376/1482/0/0,
tx=2097208/4758/0/0
    FGVMEVQGU8XTKE11(updated 5 seconds ago):
        port9: physical/1000auto, up, rx-bytes/packets/dropped/errors=453013/1151/0/0,
tx=1408259/3336/0/0
    FGVMEVECFB0ZBBDC(updated 3 seconds ago):
        port9: physical/1000auto, up, rx-bytes/packets/dropped/errors=416231/998/0/0,
tx=205476/656/0/0
MONDEV stats:
    FGVMEVU7FZZYAIE7(updated 5 seconds ago):
        port1: physical/1000auto, up, rx-bytes/packets/dropped/errors=931919/2322/0/0,
tx=960/16/0/0
        port3: physical/1000auto, up, rx-bytes/packets/dropped/errors=931919/2322/0/0,
tx=960/16/0/0
    FGVMEVQGU8XTKE11(updated 5 seconds ago):
        port1: physical/1000auto, up, rx-bytes/packets/dropped/errors=657294/1790/0/0,
tx=360/6/0/0
        port3: physical/1000auto, up, rx-bytes/packets/dropped/errors=657294/1790/0/0,
tx=360/6/0/0
    FGVMEVECFB0ZBBDC(updated 3 seconds ago):
        port1: physical/1000auto, up, rx-bytes/packets/dropped/errors=3254/36/0/0,
tx=0/0/0/0
        port3: physical/1000auto, up, rx-bytes/packets/dropped/errors=3254/36/0/0,
tx=0/0/0/0

Master: FG-B              , FGVMEVU7FZZYAIE7, cluster index = 0   → master HA unit
Slave : FG-C              , FGVMEVQGU8XTKE11, cluster index = 1
Slave : FG-D              , FGVMEVECFB0ZBBDC, cluster index = 2
number of vcluster: 1
vcluster 1: work 169.254.0.1
Master: FGVMEVU7FZZYAIE7, operating cluster index = 0
Slave : FGVMEVECFB0ZBBDC, operating cluster index = 2
Slave : FGVMEVQGU8XTKE11, operating cluster index = 1
```

Sometimes, during the synchronization, you may encounter problems. The first thing you should verify is the HA checksum. These should be the same on all cluster members.

Example 6.3

```
FG-B # diagnose sys ha checksum show
is_manage_master()=1, is_root_master()=1
debugzone
global: 37 5b cb 67 fe 58 17 ad 4f 68 bd 2e ca 22 42 e4
root: 38 3f c9 b8 f4 56 82 59 e7 41 47 b8 98 34 b5 ac
all: da 48 26 98 48 55 44 84 34 ac bd d4 3b ab b0 59
```

```
checksum
global: 37 5b cb 67 fe 58 17 ad 4f 68 bd 2e ca 22 42 e4
root:   38 3f c9 b8 f4 56 82 59 e7 41 47 b8 98 34 b5 ac
all:    da 48 26 98 48 55 44 84 34 ac bd d4 3b ab b0 59

FG-B #
```

In case you have more HA groups, you can check the output from the below command. It provides information about HA cluster members, per each group.

Example 6.4

```
FG-B # diagnose sys ha dump-by group
            HA information.
group-id=0, group-name='GR1'

gmember_nr=3
'FGVMEVECFB0ZBBDC': ha_ip_idx=2, hb_packet_version=4, last_hb_jiffies=90592, linkfails=0,
weight/o=0/0
        hbdev_nr=1: port9(mac=000c..f2, last_hb_jiffies=90592, hb_lost=0),
'FGVMEVQGU8XTKE11': ha_ip_idx=1, hb_packet_version=4, last_hb_jiffies=90598, linkfails=0,
weight/o=0/0
        hbdev_nr=1: port9(mac=000c..21, last_hb_jiffies=90598, hb_lost=0),
'FGVMEVU7FZZYAIE7': ha_ip_idx=0, hb_packet_version=4, last_hb_jiffies=0, linkfails=0,
weight/o=0/0

vcluster_nr=1
vcluster_0: start_time=1541974108(2018-11-11 14:08:28),
state/o/chg_time=2(work)/2(work)/1541974128(2018-11-11 14:08:48)
    mondev: port1(prio=50,is_aggr=0,status=1) port3(prio=50,is_aggr=0,status=1)
    'FGVMEVECFB0ZBBDC': ha_prio/o=2/2, link_failure=0, pingsvr_failure=0, flag=0x00000000,
uptime/reset_cnt=0/0
    'FGVMEVQGU8XTKE11': ha_prio/o=1/1, link_failure=0, pingsvr_failure=0, flag=0x00000000,
uptime/reset_cnt=540/0
    'FGVMEVU7FZZYAIE7': ha_prio/o=0/0, link_failure=0, pingsvr_failure=0, flag=0x00000001,
uptime/reset_cnt=789/0

FG-B #
```

Using debug commands, you can also monitor the communication between HA cluster members such as: deletions, re-election, etc.

Example 6.5

```
diagnose debug console timestamp enable
diagnose debug application hatalk -1
diagnose debug application hasync -1
diagnose debug enable
```

Example 6.6

```
2018-11-11 14:27:39 send udp packet to all peers: type=21(hastats), len=392
2018-11-11 14:27:40 member 'FGVMEVQGU8XTKE11' lost heartbeat on hbdev 'port9': now=114829, last_hb_jiffies+timeout=114426+400=114826
2018-11-11 14:27:40 lost member 'FGVMEVQGU8XTKE11' heartbeat, delete it
2018-11-11 14:27:40 deleting gmember 'FGVMEVQGU8XTKE11'
2018-11-11 14:27:40 vcluster_0: deleting vmember 'FGVMEVQGU8XTKE11'
2018-11-11 14:27:40 vcluster_0: reelect=1, delete-vmember
2018-11-11 14:27:40 cfg_changed is set to 1: hatalk_del_member
2018-11-11 14:27:40 vcluster_0: reelect=0, hatalk_vcluster_timer_func
2018-11-11 14:27:40 vcluster_0: 'FGVMEVU7FZZYAIE7' is elected as the cluster master of 2 members
2018-11-11 14:27:40 vcluster_0: state changed, 2(work)->2(work)
2018-11-11 14:27:40 vcluster_0: work_as_master immediately
```

6.2 Virtual Router Routing Protocol (VRRP)

Compared to FGCP, the number of available commands to perform VRRP troubleshooting is limited. VRRP offers less functionality but it can perform the functionality of a First Hop Redundancy Protocol in case you have different firewall models.

Starting from the design presented below I go through some useful commands to figure out if there is any issue.

Figure 6.1

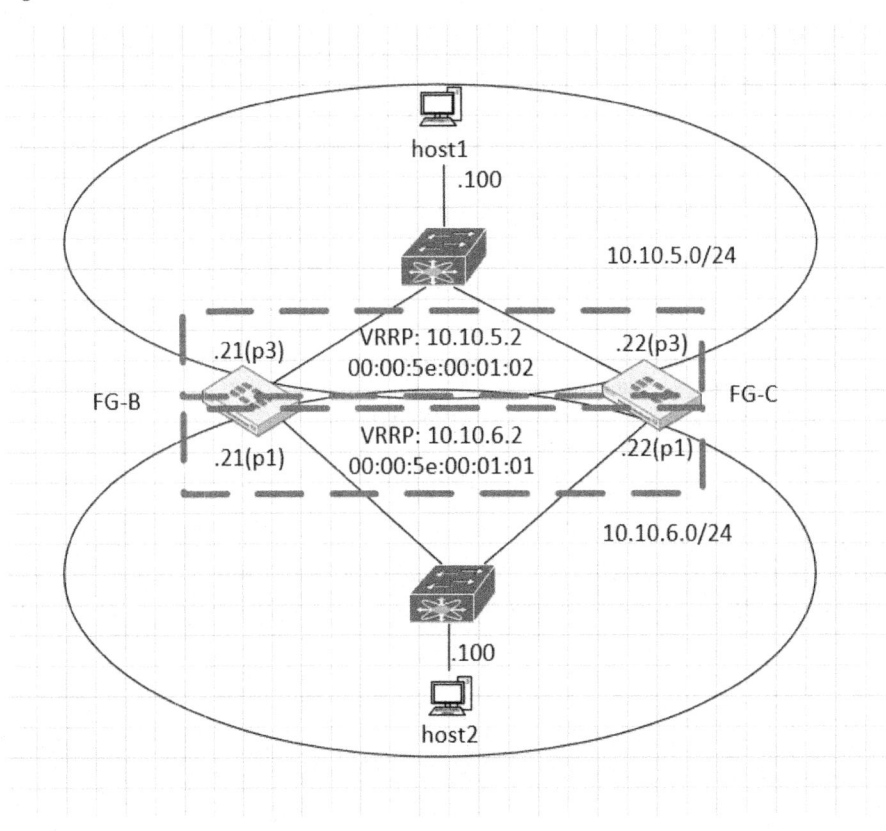

[Figure 6.1: Network diagram showing host1 (.100) on 10.10.5.0/24 network connected via a switch to FG-B (.21(p3)) and FG-C (.22(p3)) with VRRP: 10.10.5.2, 00:00:5e:00:01:02. FG-B (.21(p1)) and FG-C (.22(p1)) connect to 10.10.6.0/24 network with VRRP: 10.10.6.2, 00:00:5e:00:01:01, leading to host2 (.100) via a switch.]

Below you can see the current status. FG-B is the master with priority of 200. You can see the virtual MAC which should be in the ARP table on host2.

Example 6.7

```
FG-B # get router info vrrp
Interface: port1, primary IP address: 10.10.6.21
  UseVMAC: 1, SoftSW: 0, BrPortIdx: 0, PromiscCount: 1
  HA mode: master (0:2)
  VRID: 1
    vrip: 10.10.6.2, priority: 200 (200,0), state: MASTER
    adv_interval: 1, preempt: 1, start_time: 3
    vrmac: 00:00:5e:00:01:01 → virtual MAC which you should see on the host2
    vrdst: 10.10.6.100
```

```
      vrgrp: 1

Interface: port3, primary IP address: 10.10.5.21
  UseVMAC: 1, SoftSW: 0, BrPortIdx: 0, PromiscCount: 1
  HA mode: master (0:2)
  VRID: 2
    vrip: 10.10.5.2, priority: 200 (200,0), state: MASTER
    adv_interval: 1, preempt: 1, start_time: 3
    vrmac: 00:00:5e:00:01:02  → virtual MAC which you should see on the host1
    vrdst: 10.10.5.100
    vrgrp: 2
```

FG-C is the backup with priority 100. You can see the same virtual MAC assigned to the master which should be in the ARP table on host1.

Example 6.8

```
FG-C # get router info vrrp
Interface: port1, primary IP address: 10.10.6.22
  UseVMAC: 1, SoftSW: 0, BrPortIdx: 0, PromiscCount: 0
  HA mode: master (0:2)
  VRID: 1
    vrip: 10.10.6.2, priority: 100 (100,0), state: BACKUP
    adv_interval: 1, preempt: 1, start_time: 3
    vrmac: 00:00:5e:00:01:01→ virtual MAC which is currently assigned to the MASTER
    vrdst: 10.10.6.100
    vrgrp: 1

Interface: port3, primary IP address: 10.10.5.22
  UseVMAC: 1, SoftSW: 0, BrPortIdx: 0, PromiscCount: 0
  HA mode: master (0:2)
  VRID: 2
    vrip: 10.10.5.2, priority: 100 (100,0), state: BACKUP
    adv_interval: 1, preempt: 1, start_time: 3
    vrmac: 00:00:5e:00:01:02 → virtual MAC which is currently assigned to the MASTER
    vrdst: 10.10.5.100
    vrgrp: 2

FG-C #
```

When you ping from host1 the virtual IP 10.10.5.2 (default gateway) the master sends ICMP reply.

Example 6.9

```
[student@host1 ~]$ ping gateway
PING gateway (10.10.5.2) 56(84) bytes of data.   → ping virtual IP
64 bytes from gateway (10.10.5.2): icmp_seq=1 ttl=255 time=0.662 ms
64 bytes from gateway (10.10.5.2): icmp_seq=2 ttl=255 time=0.370 ms
64 bytes from gateway (10.10.5.2): icmp_seq=3 ttl=255 time=0.383 ms
^C
--- gateway ping statistics ---
3 packets transmitted, 3 received, 0% packet loss, time 2001ms
rtt min/avg/max/mdev = 0.370/0.471/0.662/0.137 ms
```

As shown by its ARP table, host1 learned the real and virtual MAC addresses:

Example 6.10

```
[student@host1 ~]$ arp
Address            HWtype   HWaddress           Flags Mask    Iface
10.10.5.21         ether    00:0c:29:73:0a:8c   C             ens33
gateway            ether    00:00:5e:00:01:02   C             ens33   →
MASTER's MAC address
[student@localhost ~]$
```

7 Load Balancing

FortiGate can work as a load balancer. This feature is implemented as an extension of destination NAT (DNAT). You can either do one-to-one mapping called static, or you can select one-to-many option as well.

Below there is a VIP (10.10.6.100) configured as a destination object in the firewall policy. Host1 initiates the connection to the VIP and based on the load balancing method, the traffic is forwarded to host2 or hots3.

Figure 7.1

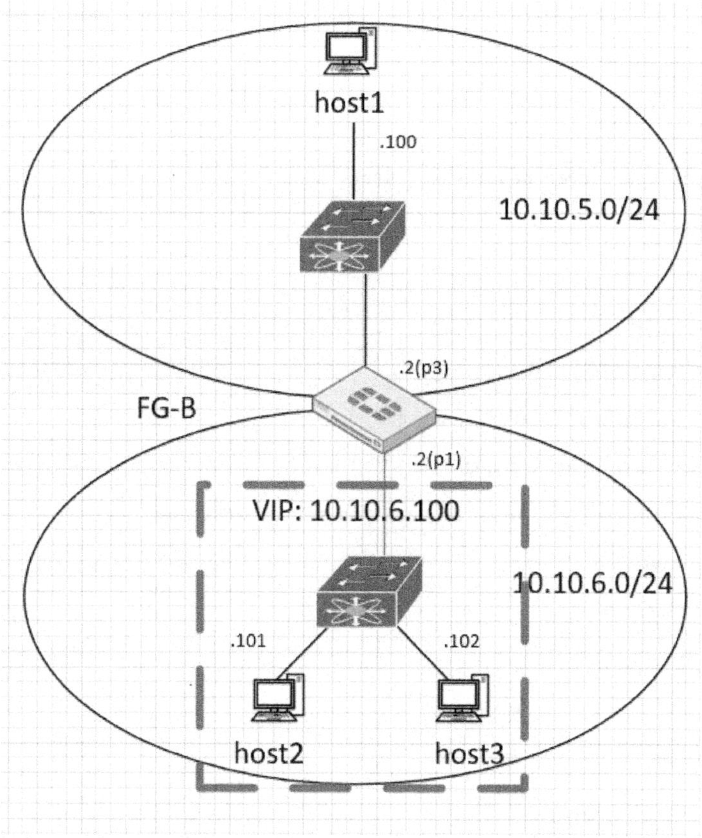

On FG-B there is a ldb-monitor, type http in this case, which monitors the availability of host2 and host3:

Example 7.1

```
FG-B # get firewall ldb-monitor
== [ LB-MONITOR ]
name: LB-MONITOR    type: http    interval: 10    timeout: 2    retry: 3    port: 80    http-get:
/    http-match: host    http-max-redirects: 0

FG-B #
```

The number of health check packets sent to the real servers shows how many servers went from down to up state and vice versa. In the below example we see two servers went up.

Example 7.2

```
FG-B # diagnose firewall vip realserver healthcheck stats show


FG-B # vip: VIP-test1
---------------------------
   time since last status change: 42951032
   num of successful checks since last status change:    260
   num of failed checks since last status change: 0
   num of times server up->down:          0 <- it means no server went down
   num of times server down->up:          2
   num of times server failovers: 0
   num of ping detects performed: 0
   num of failed ping detects:            0
   num of tcp detects performed:          0
   num of failed tcp detects:             0
   num of http detects performed: 1082
   num of failed http detects:            815
```

There are more details about each VIP and its real servers in the below diagnose command output. Both servers are up and running:

Example 7.3

```
FG-B # diagnose firewall vip realserver list
alloc=3

--------------------------------

vf=0 name=VIP-test1/1 class=4 type=1 10.10.6.100:(80-80), protocol=6    <- VIP details

total=2 alive=2 power=2 ptr=4294938466 <- number of real servers

ip=10.10.6.101-10.10.6.101/80 adm_status=0 holddown_interval=300 max_connections=0 weight=1
option=01

    alive=1 total=1 enable=00000001 alive=00000001 power=1

    src_sz=0

    id=0 status=up ks=0 us=0 events=1 bytes=11480 rtt=0  <- status of real server (up)

ip=10.10.6.102-10.10.6.102/80 adm_status=0 holddown_interval=300 max_connections=0 weight=1
option=01

    alive=1 total=1 enable=00000001 alive=00000001 power=1

    src_sz=0

    id=0 status=up ks=0 us=0 events=1 bytes=2642 rtt=0   <- status of real server (up)

FG-B #
```

From the **diagnose sniffer** command you can get the final confirmation that there are no problems in the communication between FG-B and the real servers. There is completed TCP 3-way handshake to one of these servers. It means that the server listens on port 80 and the communication is not blocked:

Example 7.4

```
FG-B # diagnose sniffer packet any 'host 10.10.6.102' 4 a
interfaces=[any]
filters=[host 10.10.6.102]
2.838167 port1 out 10.10.6.2.16573 -> 10.10.6.102.80: syn 1853128957
2.839175 port1 in 10.10.6.102.80 -> 10.10.6.2.16573: syn 2202768714 ack 1853128958
2.839263 port1 out 10.10.6.2.16573 -> 10.10.6.102.80: ack 2202768715
2.839556 port1 out 10.10.6.2.16573 -> 10.10.6.102.80: psh 1853128958 ack 2202768715
...
10 packets received by filter
0 packets dropped by kernel

FG-B #
```

By taking the server down we can see the difference in the **diagnose** command output. This action has been noticed by the FG-B:

Example 7.5

```
FG-B # diagnose firewall vip realserver healthcheck stats show
FG-B # vip: VIP-test1

  time since last status change: 42949821
  num of successful checks since last status change:      14
  num of failed checks since last status change: 42
  num of times server up->down:          1 <- one real server went down
  num of times server down->up:          2
  num of times server failovers: 0
  num of ping detects performed: 0
  num of failed ping detects:            0
```

```
num of tcp detects performed:           0
num of failed tcp detects:              0
num of http detects performed: 1268
num of failed http detects:             860
```

The real server 10.10.6.103 (host3) status is down:

Example 7.6

```
FG-B # diagnose firewall vip realserver list
alloc=3
-----------------------------
vf=0 name=VIP-test1/1 class=4 type=1 10.10.6.100:(80-80), protocol=6    <- VIP details
total=2 alive=1 power=1 ptr=4294938466
ip=10.10.6.101-10.10.6.101/80 adm_status=0 holddown_interval=300 max_connections=0 weight=1 option=01
    alive=1 total=1 enable=00000001 alive=00000001 power=1
    src_sz=0
    id=0 status=up ks=0 us=0 events=1 bytes=11480 rtt=0   <- status of real server (up)
ip=10.10.6.102-10.10.6.102/80 adm_status=0 holddown_interval=300 max_connections=0 weight=1 option=01
    alive=0 total=1 enable=00000001 alive=00000000 power=0
    src_sz=0
    id=0 status=down ks=0 us=0 events=2 bytes=2642 rtt=0   <- status of real server (down)

FG-B #
```

When I capture the traffic between FG-B and host3, I can see the RST coming from the server. It confirms the web service on host3 is down, which means port TCP/80 is now closed:

Example 7.7

```
FG-B # diagnose sniffer packet any 'host 10.10.6.102' 4 a
interfaces=[any]
filters=[host 10.10.6.102]
0.940208 port1 in arp who-has 10.10.6.2 tell 10.10.6.102
6.040719 port1 out 10.10.6.2.16599 -> 10.10.6.102.80: syn 1404325277
6.041556 port1 in 10.10.6.102.80 -> 10.10.6.2.16599: rst 0 ack 1404325278 <- the real server sends RST
8.064013 port1 out 10.10.6.2.16601 -> 10.10.6.102.80: syn 325532802
8.064874 port1 in 10.10.6.102.80 -> 10.10.6.2.16601: rst 0 ack 325532803
10.088179 port1 out 10.10.6.2.16602 -> 10.10.6.102.80: syn 3181361552
10.089056 port1 in 10.10.6.102.80 -> 10.10.6.2.16602: rst 0 ack 3181361553
^C
10 packets received by filter
0 packets dropped by kernel
```

8 Admin access

Administrative access is critical, and any issue should be solved quickly. Make sure the user is configured properly on FortiGate or on the remote server, depending on the method of authentication. For two factor authentications, such as token, use NTP server. When VDOMs are enabled double check that the admin has proper privileges.

To see a list of logged in administrators, you can use following command:

Example 8.1

```
FG-A # get system admin list

username    local     device                     vdom    profile       remote
started

admin       http      port3:7.2.3.254:80         root    super_admin   7.2.3.10:55818
2020-04-03  13:18:07

admin       ssh       port3:7.2.3.254:22         root    super_admin   7.2.3.10:55826
2020-04-03  13:18:28

user1       http      port3:7.2.3.254:80         root    prof_admin    7.2.3.10:55839
2020-04-03  13:19:18

admin       telnet    port3:7.2.3.254:23         root    super_admin   7.2.3.10:55881
2020-04-03  13:21:41


FG-A #
```

8.1 Local-in Policy

Local-in policy is a separate policy list which controls a local traffic sent from and to FortiGate. By default, the list is empty and there is an implicit permit. Once you add a policy it may impact management access, routing protocols communication (like the BGP problem described in section 5.3), etc.

As a demonstration, I have added one local-in policy which blocks telnet access:

Example 8.2

```
FG-A # show firewall local-in-policy
config firewall local-in-policy
    edit 1
        set intf "port3"
        set srcaddr "LOC-WIN"
        set dstaddr "all"
        set service "TELNET"
        set schedule "always"
    next
end

FG-A #
```

The user is not able to access the console via telnet, even if the protocol is enabled on the interface. **Diagnose debug flow** shows the reason:

Example 8.3

```
id=20085 trace_id=1033 func=print_pkt_detail line=5517 msg="vd-root:0 received a packet(proto=6, 7.2.3.10:56008->7.2.3.254:23) from port3. flag [S], seq 1981044830, ack 0, win 8192"

id=20085 trace_id=1033 func=init_ip_session_common line=5682 msg="allocate a new session-00274568"

id=20085 trace_id=1033 func=vf_ip_route_input_common line=2591 msg="find a route: flag=84000000 gw-7.2.3.254 via root"

id=20085 trace_id=1033 func=fw_local_in_handler line=410 msg="iprope_in_check() check failed on policy 1, drop"
```

8.2 Trusted Source

One of the features I recommend is a trusted source. You set source IP address or IP subnet for each administrator. Once someone tries to login from a source IP which is not permitted, following log entry is generated:

Example 8.4

```
FG-A # execute log filter category 1   <- category '1' means event
FG-A # execute log display
...
4: date=2020-04-03 time=13:32:52 logid="0100032002" type="event" subtype="system"
level="alert" vd="root" eventtime=1585945971 logdesc="Admin login failed" sn="0"
user="user2" ui="http(7.2.3.10)" method="http" srcip=7.2.3.10 dstip=7.2.3.254 action="login"
status="failed" reason="ip_blocked" msg="Administrator user2 login failed from
http(7.2.3.10) because of blocked IP"
```

The message is clear enough to understand the root cause.

8.3 HTTPS access vs SSL-VPN

When you enable management access and SSL-VPN on the same interface (and the same TCP port), SSL VPN has higher priority. You will not be able to access the GUI remotely.

9 Hardware (CPU, memory, disk, flash)

Diagnosing hardware issues or overutilization is an important part of the troubleshooting you may be dealing with. Not all the problems are caused by mis-configuration.

9.1 Hardware status

Let's start from the hardware overview, on the FortiGate VM:

Example 9.1

```
FG-A # get hardware status
Model name: FortiGate-VM64
ASIC version: not available
CPU: Intel(R) Core(TM) i7-2670QM CPU @ 2.20GHz
Number of CPUs: 1
RAM: 1003 MB
Compact Flash: 2056 MB /dev/sda
Hard disk: 30720 MB /dev/sdb
USB Flash: not available

FG-A #
```

And then on the popular appliance model 1500D:

Example 9.2

```
FG-A (global) # get hardware status
Model name: FortiGate-1500D
```

```
ASIC version: CP8

ASIC SRAM: 64M

CPU: Intel(R) Xeon(R) CPU E5-1650 v2 @ 3.50GHz

Number of CPUs: 12

RAM: 16064 MB

Compact Flash: 30653 MB /dev/sda

Hard disk: 228936 MB /dev/sdb

USB Flash: not available

Network Card chipset: Broadcom 570x Tigon3 Ethernet Adapter (rev.0x5717100)

Network Card chipset: FortiASIC NP6 Adapter (rev.)


FG-A (global) #
```

9.2 Network Interface Card

In case of connectivity problems, you can verify the port state, and check the interface errors (VM and appliance):

Example 9.3

```
FG-A # get hardware nic port1
Name:              port1
Driver:            e1000
Version:           7.3.21-k8-NAPI
FW version:        N/A
Bus:               0000:02:00.0
Hwaddr:            00:0c:23:a3:33:33
Permanent Hwaddr:00:0c:23:a3:33:33
State:             up
Link:              up
```

Mtu:	1500
Supported:	auto 10half 10full 100half 100full 1000full
Advertised:	auto 10half 10full 100half 100full 1000full
Speed:	1000full
Auto:	enabled
Rx packets:	59528
Rx bytes:	54453498
Rx compressed:	0
Rx dropped:	0
Rx errors:	0
Rx Length err:	0
Rx Buf overflow:	0
Rx Crc err:	0
Rx Frame err:	0
Rx Fifo overrun:	0
Rx Missed packets:	0
Tx packets:	42763
Tx bytes:	25593979
Tx compressed:	0
Tx dropped:	0
Tx errors:	0
Tx Aborted err:	0
Tx Carrier err:	0
Tx Fifo overrun:	0
Tx Heartbeat err:	0
Tx Window err:	0
Multicasts:	0
Collisions:	0

Example 9.4

```
FG-A (global) # get hardware nic port34
Description       :FortiASIC NP6 Adapter
Driver Name       :FortiASIC Unified NPU Driver
Name              :np6_0
PCI Slot          :0000:09:00.0
irq               :34
Board             :FGT1500D
SN                :FGXXXXXXXXXXX
Major ID          :3
Minor ID          :0
lif id            :17
lif oid           :147
netdev oid        :147
netdev flags      :1903
Current_HWaddr    00:09:0f:03:33:23
Permanent_HWaddr  70:3c:a2:03:33:33
phy name          :port34
bank_id           :1
phy_addr          :0x19
lane              :1
flags             :804006
sw_port           :2
sw_np_port        :14
vid_phy[6]        :[0x13][0x4d][0x00][0x00][0x00][0x00]
vid_fwd[6]        :[0x00][0x4c][0x00][0x00][0x00][0x00]
oid_fwd[6]        :[0x00][0xbd][0x00][0x00][0x00][0x00]
========== Link Status ==========
Admin             :up
```

```
netdev status      :up
autonego_setting:0
link_setting       :1
link_speed         :10000
link_duplex        :1
Speed              :10000
Duplex             :Full
link_status        :Up
rx_link_status     :0
int_phy_link       :0
local_fault        :0
local_warning      :0
remote_fault       :0
============ Counters ===========
rx_error           :20
rx_crc_error       :1
rx_carrier         :0
rx_oversize        :0
rx_undersize       :0
tx_collision       :0
Rx Pkts            :5227201254529
Rx Bytes           :3961535471816449
Tx Pkts            :5253408976817
Tx Bytes           :3883285272144822
Host Rx Pkts       :106620511735
Host Rx Bytes      :29022301200029
Host Rx dropped    :0
Host Tx Pkts       :97712488169
Host Tx Bytes      :29776365795453
```

```
Host Tx dropped :0
sw_rx_pkts         :5227201292067
sw_rx_bytes        :3961535502780310
sw_tx_pkts         :5253409015022
sw_tx_bytes        :3883285304984801
sw_rx_mc_pkts      :8138073002
sw_rx_bc_pkts      :9955629691
sw_in_drop_pkts    :0
sw_out_drop_pkts   :0
sw_np_rx_pkts      :5253730241372
sw_np_rx_bytes     :3904722115300076
sw_np_tx_pkts      :5357700267394
sw_np_tx_bytes     :4141423522685514
sw_np_rx_mc_pkts   :2124450
sw_np_rx_bc_pkts   :603413846
sw_np_in_drop_pkts :8
sw_np_out_drop_pkts:0
```

9.3 Network Processor

When your model has more Network Processors (ASIC NP) you should know which ports are offloaded to which NP. Try to distribute the workload as equally as possible.

Example 9.5

```
FG-A (global) # get hardware npu np6 port-list
Chip    XAUI  Ports         Max    Cross-chip
                            Speed  offloading
------  ----  -------       -----  ----------
np6_0   0     port1         1G     Yes
```

	0	port5	1G	Yes
	0	port17	1G	Yes
	0	port21	1G	Yes
	0	port33	10G	Yes
	1	port2	1G	Yes
	1	port6	1G	Yes
	1	port18	1G	Yes
	1	port22	1G	Yes
	1	port34	10G	Yes
	2	port3	1G	Yes
	2	port7	1G	Yes
	2	port19	1G	Yes
	2	port23	1G	Yes
	2	port35	10G	Yes
	3	port4	1G	Yes
	3	port8	1G	Yes
	3	port20	1G	Yes
	3	port24	1G	Yes
	3	port36	10G	Yes
------	----	-------	-----	----------
np6_1	0	port9	1G	Yes
	0	port13	1G	Yes
	0	port25	1G	Yes
	0	port29	1G	Yes
	0	port37	10G	Yes
	1	port10	1G	Yes
	1	port14	1G	Yes
	1	port26	1G	Yes
	1	port30	1G	Yes

```
     1    port38         10G   Yes
     2    port11         1G    Yes
     2    port15         1G    Yes
     2    port27         1G    Yes
     2    port31         1G    Yes
     2    port39         10G   Yes
     3    port12         1G    Yes
     3    port16         1G    Yes
     3    port28         1G    Yes
     3    port32         1G    Yes
     3    port40         10G   Yes
------ ---- -------      ----- ----------

FG-A (global) #
```

The models 900d, 1000d and 1200d do not have Integrated Switch Fabric (ISF). You cannot setup a Link Aggregation (LAG) by selecting interfaces assigned to different NPs. LAG is supported only for interfaces within the same NP. Lower models may have only one NP, while higher models, such as 1500d, have ISF which allows to setup LAGs with interfaces allocated to different NPs.

9.4 Transceiver

When you have SPF/SPF+ use the below command to check the temperature, voltage, alarms or warnings.

Example 9.6

```
FG-A (global) # get system interface transceiver
Interface port1 - Transceiver is not detected.
```

```
...
Interface port5 - SFP/SFP+
  Vendor Name   :              FINISAR CORP.
  Part No.      :              FTLF1328P3DAS
  Serial No.    :              XXXXXXX
Interface port6 - Transceiver is not detected.
Interface port8 - Transceiver is not detected.
...
                                  Optical      Optical      Optical
SFP/SFP+        Temperature  Voltage   Tx Bias      Tx Power     Rx Power
Interface       (Celsius)    (Volts)   (mA)         (dBm)        (dBm)
-----------     -----------  --------  -----------  -----------  -----------
port5           37.7         3.30      19.27        -5.5         -3.3
...
  ++ : high alarm, + : high warning, - : low warning, -- : low alarm, ? : suspect.

FG-A (global) #
```

9.5 System performance

The system performance should be monitored in order to know when you hit the device limits and enter to conserve mode. The first output is from the FortiGate VM:

Example 9.7

```
FG-A # get system performance status
CPU states: 0% user 0% system 0% nice 100% idle 0% iowait 0% irq 0% softirq
CPU0 states: 0% user 0% system 0% nice 100% idle 0% iowait 0% irq 0% softirq
Memory: 1027572k total, 732380k used (71.3%), 181016k free (17.6%), 114176k freeable (11.1%)
```

```
Average network usage: 11 / 10 kbps in 1 minute, 16 / 45 kbps in 10 minutes, 9 / 22 kbps in
30 minutes

Average sessions: 26 sessions in 1 minute, 33 sessions in 10 minutes, 29 sessions in 30
minutes

Average session setup rate: 0 sessions per second in last 1 minute, 0 sessions per second in
last 10 minutes, 0 sessions per second in last 30 minutes

Virus caught: 0 total in 1 minute

IPS attacks blocked: 0 total in 1 minute

Uptime: 0 days,  5 hours,  16 minutes


FG-A #
```

And below, the one from the physical device:

Example 9.8

```
FG-A (global) # get system performance status

CPU states: 1% user 7% system 0% nice 92% idle 0% iowait 0% irq 0% softirq

CPU0 states: 0% user 0% system 0% nice 93% idle 0% iowait 7% irq 0% softirq

CPU1 states: 0% user 0% system 0% nice 100% idle 0% iowait 0% irq 0% softirq

CPU2 states: 0% user 2% system 0% nice 97% idle 0% iowait 0% irq 1% softirq

CPU3 states: 0% user 2% system 0% nice 98% idle 0% iowait 0% irq 0% softirq

CPU4 states: 0% user 1% system 0% nice 98% idle 0% iowait 0% irq 1% softirq

CPU5 states: 3% user 17% system 0% nice 80% idle 0% iowait 0% irq 0% softirq

CPU6 states: 4% user 25% system 0% nice 70% idle 0% iowait 0% irq 1% softirq

CPU7 states: 2% user 12% system 0% nice 86% idle 0% iowait 0% irq 0% softirq

CPU8 states: 0% user 2% system 0% nice 97% idle 0% iowait 0% irq 1% softirq

CPU9 states: 3% user 24% system 0% nice 73% idle 0% iowait 0% irq 0% softirq

CPU10 states: 4% user 3% system 0% nice 93% idle 0% iowait 0% irq 0% softirq

CPU11 states: 0% user 0% system 0% nice 100% idle 0% iowait 0% irq 0% softirq

Memory: 16449944k total, 3758816k used (22%), 12691128k free (78%), 40348k buffers
```

Average network usage: 2702214 / 2699634 kbps in 1 minute, 2723314 / 2720427 kbps in 10 minutes, 2740728 / 2737566 kbps in 30 minutes

Average sessions: 82596 sessions in 1 minute, 84890 sessions in 10 minutes, 83121 sessions in 30 minutes

Average session setup rate: 1243 sessions per second in last 1 minute, 1397 sessions per second in last 10 minutes, 1401 sessions per second in last 30 minutes

Average NPU sessions: 35194 sessions in last 1 minute, 35939 sessions in last 10 minutes, 36515 sessions in last 30 minutes

Average nTurbo sessions: 0 sessions in last 1 minute, 0 sessions in last 10 minutes, 0 sessions in last 30 minutes

Virus caught: 0 total in 1 minute

IPS attacks blocked: 0 total in 1 minute

Uptime: 49 days, 4 hours, 17 minutes

FG-A (global) #
```

## 9.6 Sys top

When you notice a high CPU or memory usage you can check which process uses most of the resources. The first command shows summary information with the number of instances of the same process.

Example 9.9

```
FG-A # diagnose sys top-summary
    CPU [|||||||||||||||||||||||||||||||||||||||] 100.0%
    Mem [|||||||||||||||||||||||||||||||] 83.0%   833M/1003M
    Processes: 20 (running=1 sleeping=94)

      PID   RSS   ^CPU% MEM%   FDS   TIME+ NAME
    * 138   7M   0.0   0.7   12   00:00.10 uploadd
      139   22M   0.0   2.3   52   00:02.54 miglogd [x2] <- there are two processes
```
```

```
140       6M      0.0   0.7    8   00:00.00  kmiglogd
141      59M      0.0   5.9   22   00:27.40  httpsd [x5]
143       7M      0.0   0.7    8   00:00.00  mingetty
144       7M      0.0   0.7    8   00:00.00  mingetty
145       7M      0.0   0.7   11   00:06.89  vmtoolsd
146      10M      0.0   1.1   74   00:04.26  ipsmonitor [x2]
147       7M      0.0   0.7   11   00:08.83  merged_daemons
148       9M      0.0   0.9   15   00:00.10  fnbamd
149       7M      0.0   0.7   12   00:00.15  fclicense
150      26M      0.0   2.7   25   00:05.63  forticron
151      10M      0.0   1.0   17   00:00.12  forticldd
152       9M      0.0   1.0   41   00:00.70  authd
153       9M      0.0   0.9   22   00:00.20  foauthd
154       6M      0.0   0.7    9   00:00.00  httpclid
155      29M      0.0   3.0   15   00:00.70  reportd
156       8M      0.0   0.8   22   00:00.49  voipd
157       7M      0.0   0.7    8   00:00.00  getty
158      12M      0.0   1.2   15   00:01.30  updated
CPU [||                 ]   6.6%
Mem [|||||||||||||||||||||||||||||||      ]  83.0%   834M/1003M
Processes: 20 (running=2 sleeping=93)
```

The below version of the command presents every process separately:

Example 9.10

```
FG-A # diagnose sys top
Run Time:  0 days, 5 hours and 16 minutes
0U, 0N, 0S, 100I, 0WA, 0HI, 0SI, 0ST; 1003T, 175F
          httpsd      2684      S      0.4    2.8
```

```
       zebos_launcher    125    S    0.4    0.7
             dnsproxy    165    S    0.0    7.2
              pyfcgid   2618    S    0.0    4.5
              pyfcgid   2617    S    0.0    4.5
              pyfcgid   2615    S    0.0    4.2
               httpsd    183    S    0.0    4.0  <- management access (GUI)
               httpsd    187    S    0.0    3.9  <- management access (GUI)
              cmdbsvr    118    S    0.0    3.0
              reportd    155    S    0.0    2.9
               newcli   2367    S    0.0    2.9
            forticron    150    S    0.0    2.6
              sslvpnd    463    S    0.0    2.5
              pyfcgid   2619    S    0.0    2.4
               httpsd    141    S    0.0    2.4
              miglogd    139    S    0.0    2.2
               cw_acd    168    R    0.0    2.2
               newcli   2645    S    0.0    2.0
               newcli   2712    R    0.0    1.8
               httpsd    182    S    0.0    1.5
```

9.7 Flash and disk

The flash and disk errors are very dangerous as they can impact the system stability. Before you plan to reboot the device make sure you check the flash status before. The same is recommended when you plan to upgrade the firmware. In case you have HA cluster, check all devices.

Example 9.11

```
FG-A (global) # diagnose sys flash list
```

```
Partition  Image                              TotalSize(KB)  Used(KB)  Use%  Active
1          FG1K5D-X.XX-FW-buildXXXX-17XXXX          253871     54724   22%   Yes
2          FG1K5D-HQIP-3.6.9-build2933               63461     35041   55%   No
3          EXDB-1.00000                           30249764     46196    0%   No
Image build at Aug 26 2019 22:31:48 for bXXXX
```

On models with internal hard drive you can check disks and partitions:

Example 9.12

```
FG-A (global) # execute disk list

Disk HDD1            ref:  16  223.6GB    type: SSD [ATA SSDSC2BR123G7] dev: /dev/sdb
  partition ref:  17  220.1GB, 219.9GB free  mounted: Y  label: LOGUSEDXB49BC12A dev: /dev/sdb1 start: 2048

Disk HDD2            ref:  32  223.6GB    type: SSD [ATA SSDSC2BR123G7] dev: /dev/sdc
  partition ref:  33  220.1GB, 219.9GB free  mounted: N  label: WANOPTXXAC737123 dev: /dev/sdc1 start: 2048
```

Another command to verify the disk setup:

Example 9.13

```
FG-A (global) $ diag hardware deviceinfo disk

Disk Internal-0      ref: 259   29.8GB    type: SSD [ATA 32GB SATA Flash] dev: /dev/sda
  partition ref:   1  247.0MB, 194.0MB free  mounted: Y  label:   dev: /dev/sda1 start: 1
  partition ref:   2  256.0MB, 256.0MB free  mounted: N  label:   dev: /dev/sda2 start: 524289
```

```
   partition ref:    3  28.8GB,  28.8GB free  mounted: Y  label:   dev: /dev/sda3 start:
1048577


Disk HDD1            ref:  16 223.6GB    type: SSD [ATA SSDSC2BR123G7] dev: /dev/sdb

   partition ref:   17 220.1GB, 219.7GB free  mounted: Y  label: LOGUSEDXFA949123 dev:
/dev/sdb1 start: 2048


Disk HDD2            ref:  32 223.6GB    type: SSD [ATA SSDSC1BR24123] dev: /dev/sdc

   partition ref:   33 220.1GB, 219.9GB free  mounted: N  label: WANOPTXXBB000123 dev:
/dev/sdc1 start: 2048


Total available disks: 3

Max SSD disks: 2  Available storage disks: 2


FG-A (global)
```

10 Other - uncategorized

In the last chapter I gathered different useful commands which do not match any category presented earlier.

10.1 ARP

On a device in NAT mode you can check the ARP table.

Example 10.1

```
FG-A # get system arp
Address            Age(min)    Hardware Addr         Interface
7.2.3.10           0           00:0c:29:0f:12:4d     port3
7.2.3.20           0           00:0c:29:74:c6:12     port3
172.16.1.254       0           00:0c:29:3f:12:75     port1
172.16.2.254       0           00:0c:29:3f:20:7f     port2

FG-A #
```

If more details are required, such as number of ARP updates, etc., you can check an output form the **diagnose ip arp list** command:

Example 10.2

```
FG-A # diagnose ip arp list
index=5 ifname=port3 7.2.3.10 00:0c:29:0f:12:4d state=00000002 use=12 confirm=9 update=50704 ref=4

index=5 ifname=port3 7.2.3.20 00:0c:29:74:c6:12 state=00000004 use=916 confirm=3639 update=361 ref=2
```

```
index=13 ifname=root 0.0.0.0 00:00:00:00:00:00 state=00000040 use=48467 confirm=48467
update=49502 ref=1

index=3 ifname=port1 172.16.1.254 00:0c:29:3f:12:75 state=00000004 use=919 confirm=4844
update=409 ref=12

index=4 ifname=port2 172.16.2.254 00:0c:29:3f:20:7f state=00000002 use=24 confirm=643
update=12 ref=3


FG-A #
```

10.2 LAG

Link aggregation is a recommended feature in high availability environments. You should be able to check the settings and the current state of LAG.

The **diagnose netlink aggregate** command has a few options. The 'list' one shows of all LAGs with information about the status, algorithms and mode:

Example 10.3

```
FG-A (CUSTOMERA) # diagnose netlink aggregate list
List of 802.3ad link aggregation interfaces:
    1   name ae1              status up        algorithm L4   lacp-mode active
    2   name ae2              status up        algorithm L4   lacp-mode active


FG-A (CUSTOMERA) #
```

When you need investigate LAG interface, check the below command version. There are many details about each member.

Example 10.4

```
FG-A (CUSTOMERA) # diagnose netlink aggregate name ae1
```

```
LACP flags: (A|P)(S|F)(A|I)(I|O)(E|D)(E|D)
(A|P) - LACP mode is Active or Passive
(S|F) - LACP speed is Slow or Fast
(A|I) - Aggregatable or Individual
(I|O) - Port In sync or Out of sync
(E|D) - Frame collection is Enabled or Disabled
(E|D) - Frame distribution is Enabled or Disabled

status: up
npu: y
flush: n
asic helper: y <- only on models with ASICs
oid: 147
ports: 2
link-up-delay: 50ms
min-links: 1
ha: master
distribution algorithm: L4
LACP mode: active
LACP speed: slow
LACP HA: enable
aggregator ID: 4
actor key: 33
actor MAC address: 70:4c:a8:78:12:8c
partner key: 32776
partner MAC address: 00:23:04:11:22:33

slave: port13
   link status: up
```

```
link failure count: 7
permanent MAC addr: 70:4c:a5:33:22:11
LACP state: established
actor state: ASAIEE
actor port number/key/priority: 1 33 255
partner state: ASAIEE
partner port number/key/priority: 16674 32776 32768
partner system: 0 00:23:04:ee:be:01
aggregator ID: 4
speed/duplex: 10000 1
RX state: CURRENT 6
MUX state: COLLECTING_DISTRIBUTING 4

slave: port14
  link status: up
  link failure count: 8
  permanent MAC addr: 70:4c:a5:11:22:33
  LACP state: established
  actor state: ASAIEE
  actor port number/key/priority: 2 33 255
  partner state: ASAIEE
  partner port number/key/priority: 290 32776 32768
  partner system: 0 00:23:04:33:22:11
  aggregator ID: 4
  speed/duplex: 10000 1
  RX state: CURRENT 6
  MUX state: COLLECTING_DISTRIBUTING 4
```

10.3 Configuration Management Database (CMDB)

Every configuration object in use cannot be removed. A good example is an interface which should be added as a LAG member. From the GUI, on the interface page list, you can check where the interface is used. From the CLI you can verify dependencies using the following command:

Example 10.5

```
FG-A # diagnose sys cmdb refcnt show system.interface.name port3
entry used by table system.dns-server:name 'port3'
entry used by child table srcintf:name 'port3' of table firewall.policy:policyid '1'
entry used by child table dstintf:name 'port3' of table firewall.policy:policyid '2'
entry used by table firewall.local-in-policy:policyid '1'
entry used by child table input-device:name 'port3' of table router.policy:seq-num '1'

FG-A #
```

10.4 Grep

A FortiGate configuration file can be very lengthy. Using **grep** with a parameter '-f' shows only the relevant parts you may be interested in:

Example 10.6

```
FG-A # show | grep -f LOC-WIN
config firewall address
    edit "LOC-WIN"  <---
        set subnet 7.2.3.10 255.255.255.255
    next
```

```
end
config firewall local-in-policy
    edit 1
        set intf "port7"
        set srcaddr "LOC-WIN" <---
        set dstaddr "all"
        set service "TELNET"
        set schedule "always"
    next
end
config router policy
    edit 1
        set input-device "port7"
        set srcaddr "LOC-WIN" <---
        set dst "8.8.8.8/255.255.255.255"
        set protocol 6
        set gateway 8.8.8.8
        set output-device "port22"
    next
end

FG-A #
```

10.5 Crashlog

Crashlog is a type of log where information about unstable or killed processes, conserve mode are logged. In the below example you see I/O error on sda1:

Example 10.7

```
FG-A (global) $ diagnose debug crashlog read
1: 2020-02-02 07:10:58 EXT2-fs (sda1): previous I/O error to superblock detected
2: 2020-02-02 07:11:04 EXT2-fs (sda1): previous I/O error to superblock detected
3: 2020-02-02 07:11:10 EXT2-fs (sda1): previous I/O error to superblock detected
4: 2020-02-02 07:11:16 EXT2-fs (sda1): previous I/O error to superblock detected
5: 2020-02-02 07:11:22 EXT2-fs (sda1): previous I/O error to superblock detected
```

And conserve mode:

Example 10.8

```
2020-02-17 11:21:57 pages" red="39320 pages" msg="Kernel enters conserve mode"
2020-02-17 11:22:00 logdesc="Kernel leaves conserve mode" service=kernel conserve=exit
2020-02-17 11:22:00 free="108337 pages" green="58980 pages" msg="Kernel leaves conserve mode"
2020-02-17 11:22:08 logdesc="Kernel enters conserve mode" service=kernel conserve=on free="38419
```

10.6 TAC

While working on a problem with Fortinet TAC you may be asked to provide an output from **execute tac report** command. There is no output here because it is very lengthy. I recommend checking it and see what details you can find there. You may not understand everything as most of the details can be analyzed only by Fortinet TAC engineers.

Example 10.8

```
execute tac report
```

11 Index

D

diag hardware deviceinfo disk, 152
diagnose debug application hasync, 126
diagnose debug application hatalk, 126
diagnose debug application ike, 57
diagnose debug application ipsengine, 54
diagnose debug application scanunit, 51
diagnose debug application sslvpn, 81
diagnose debug application urlfilter, 48
diagnose debug console timestamp enable, 126
diagnose debug crashlog read, 160
diagnose debug flow, 21, 85
diagnose debug urlfilter, 47
diagnose firewall ippool-all stats, 29
diagnose firewall proute list, 93
diagnose firewall vip realserver healthcheck stats show, 131, 133
diagnose firewall vip realserver list, 132, 134
diagnose ip arp list, 154
diagnose ip router bgp, 113
diagnose ip router ospf, 105
diagnose netlink aggregate list, 155
diagnose netlink aggregate name, 155
diagnose sniffer packet, 16
diagnose sys cmdb refcnt show system.interface.name, 158
diagnose sys flash list, 151
diagnose sys ha checksum show, 124
diagnose sys ha dump-by group, 125
diagnose sys link-monitor status, 94
diagnose sys session filter, 15
diagnose sys session list, 13
diagnose sys top, 150
diagnose sys top-summary, 149
diagnose test application ipsmonitor, 55
diagnose vpn ike gateway list, 63
diagnose vpn tunnel list, 64

E

execute disk list, 152
execute log display, 138
execute log filter category, 138
execute router clear bgp all, 116
execute tac report, 160

G

get firewall ldb-monitor, 131
get hardware nic, 140
get hardware npu np6 port-list, 144
get hardware status, 139
get router info bgp network, 113
get router info bgp summary, 113
get router info ospf database brief, 100
get router info ospf database router lsa, 100
get router info ospf interface, 101
get router info ospf neighbor all, 98
get router info ospf neighbor detail all, 99
get router info ospf route, 102
get router info ospf status, 98
get router info protocols, 97
get router info routing-table all, 88
get router info routing-table bgp, 113
get router info routing-table database, 89
get router info vrrp, 127
get system admin list, 136
get system arp, 154
get system ha status, 123
get system interface transceiver, 146

get system performance status, 147
get system session list, 12
get system status, 122
get vpn ike gateway, 67
get vpn ipsec stats crypto, 68
get vpn ipsec tunnel details, 66
get vpn ipsec tunnel summary, 69

S

sh firewall vip, 32
show | grep -f, 158
show firewall central-snat-map, 37
show firewall local-in-policy, 137

Made in the USA
Columbia, SC
24 September 2020